Medical Clinics and Practices

Medical Clinics and Practices

Understanding How They Work and Why

Roger Gruneisen

Routledge
Taylor & Francis Group

A PRODUCTIVITY PRESS BOOK

First edition published in 2020
by Routledge/Productivity Press
52 Vanderbilt Avenue, 11th Floor New York, NY 10017
2 Park Square, Milton Park, Abingdon, Oxon OX14 4RN, UK

© 2020 by Taylor & Francis Group, LLC

Routledge/Productivity Press is an imprint of Taylor & Francis Group, an Informa business

No claim to original U.S. Government works

Printed on acid-free paper

International Standard Book Number-13: 978-1-138-34142-5 (Hardback)
International Standard Book Number-13: 978-1-138-34139-5 (Paperback)
International Standard Book Number-13: 978-0-429-44015-1 (eBook)

Library of Congress Control Number: 2019948537

**Visit the Taylor & Francis Web site at
www.taylorandfrancis.com**

Special thanks go to David Jonson JJCA for the following figures: images for Figures 8.1, 8.3, 8.7, 10.6, and 10.7; background images and marked up Figures 8.4, 8.5, 9.3, and 10.3.

Contents

About the Author

Roger Gruneisen is a healthcare operations management professional and consultant with extensive experience in Lean Six Sigma, Operations Research, organizational change, and performance improvement. Roger has a Bachelor of Science in Operations Research from the United States Military Academy and a Master of Science in Operations Management from the University of Arkansas.

After service in the U.S. Army, Roger worked for General Electric in the commercial industry before switching to healthcare operations roles. Roger's healthcare roles have taken him to work in acute and ambulatory settings in academic medicine, federal medical systems, for-profit health systems, and smaller critical access hospitals with rural health clinics. Professionally, Roger finds it extremely rewarding to have a career focused on improving the delivery of healthcare and improving the organizational decision making behind healthcare delivery.

Roger happily resides in Central Kentucky with his wife, two daughters, and two labradors.

INTRODUCTION

1

Chapter 1

Why Write this Book?

My first full-time work experience as an adult was doing what I might say was the opposite of what healthcare does. I was a combat leader in the United States Army. I left the service and found myself using my leadership skills and Operations Research background in the industrial sector. While challenging, it was not extremely fulfilling work which is how I made my way into working with the great folks in healthcare.

I am not clinical, but I have spent a great deal of time alongside and learning from physicians, nurses, medical assistants, facilities managers, housekeepers, administrators, you name it, and of course I have much more to learn. I have also spent a great deal of time with other consultants, management engineers, and analytical specialists dissecting healthcare operations, formulating recommendations, and helping to implement those recommendations into practice. From this experience, I believe the challenges and operating environment inside healthcare are more like the challenges and operating environments I faced in the Army than those I experienced in the industrial sector. People are passionate about what they do in healthcare and what they do is usually stressful. There is not always a good answer to every problem. The day to day work is not without constant variation and involves constant learning.

As mentioned, I do not have a clinical background but have helped healthcare teams to make minor, major, or drastic changes. In my work, I am occasionally challenged with the phrases "this is healthcare not manufacturing" or "you're not clinical so you won't get it." The context in which these challenges occur usually involves a team faced with making changes to how people work and realistically, people don't like change. Those phrases are typically used in a cautionary tone or on some occasions as a declaration of defiance. I agree that I am not clinical and will not know the depth of clinical challenges that clinical staff face. I agree that healthcare is not manufacturing and for many reasons should not be treated like that, though some management principles from industry do apply well in certain healthcare operations.

For the first part of my life, I knew very little about healthcare or what goes on in healthcare. I was preoccupied with other aspects of life. From this experience I can say that I do have a good understanding of what it is like to be a confused patient going through the healthcare experience. I can also say that I learned what it is like to lead teams in the most stressful, dangerous, and variable work environment – combat. From my time in industry, I learned the value of deploying management and analytical problem-solving methods.

In the more recent part of my life, from all the time spent working with clinical staff, talking to folks in healthcare, and observing how work gets done, I can now say that I have a good sense of healthcare operations, compared to those working outside healthcare and even compared to many working inside healthcare. I came to this understanding by spending a great deal of time observing work, interviewing clinical leaders, facilitating change, managing people through change, analyzing mounds of data and information on all parts of clinics, trialing different ways to explain what data meant, and sticking around to accept the outcomes of work. In short, I got a lot of time to learn the breadth of clinical operations and some depth through experience.

In order to provide a solution, help facilitate change, deliver tangible products or lead people, I believe it is critical to understand what people do, why they do it, what tools they must work with, who the people are, and what space they must work in. I wrote this book primarily to provide knowledge for other non-clinical folk that will routinely or occasionally interact in healthcare. Taking time to learn and understand the work and challenges other people face is a show of respect and it is much needed in healthcare. Whether someone is a new management engineer assigned to a clinic performance improvement team, an architect new to designing clinic space, a consultant that has spent only time in Acute Care but is transitioning to Ambulatory Care, a salesperson trying to deliver a specific solution, or even a patient that just wants to learn more of what to expect, taking time to understand what others have to do is valuable. First learning and understanding what others do will allow someone to later provide relevant solutions or personally help others to change.

This book is an introductory walkthrough about how simple clinics and medical practices operate. I am not trying to satisfy all people for all things with this book. The book is primarily intended for non-clinicians that are seeking to understand the environment, processes, and critical factors related to clinics. Even though it is not intended for clinicians, there may be plenty of value for staff experienced already in healthcare.

The book should serve as a guide to new consultants learning how to rapidly assess a clinic and provide meaningful insights back to the customer. The book should help new management engineers characterize the many differences between each clinic within the health system. The book should give sales professionals ideas on how their solution fits into a clinic's mission. The book should introduce new healthcare administrators to the operation he or she will help manage. In general, the book should help those seeking to better understand any simple clinic or medical practice operation. While this book is not comprehensive to all possibilities, variations, or benchmarks, the reader should be able to formulate a better sense of understanding of what is going on in any clinic operation they walk into, if for no other purpose than to help them carry out a more value-added conversation with those working day to day in healthcare.

Chapter 2

How to Use this Book

The book serves as a guide to understanding key aspects of any clinic the reader visits. Rather than creating a book that simply states important information about each aspect of the operation, each chapter in this book is comprised of a series of questions the reader should ask or find out the answer to when visiting a clinic. Following each question, I explain the relevance the question has or what some common operating practices might be and will occasionally indicate whether there might be a good or better practice. I provide pictures and sample data collection tables, analysis tables and graphs, sample process flows, and more to better explain my point as well as to provide the reader with tools to use.

To simplify the chapter flow, I organized the main content chapters into four sections. The first section provides high level information on clinics and associated questions. The second section questions are organized in order of how patients flow through the clinic system. The third section questions dive a little deeper into provider throughput, capacity, and space utilization. The fourth section provides additional chapters on management, communication, technology, and organizational topics.

In all, there are over 20 chapters filled with close to 100 questions. In the appendix, I included a table summary of all the questions organized by chapter topic. The information is summarized so that the reader can use the table as a checklist or turn it into a questionnaire each time the reader goes and experiences a clinic.

I recommend that the reader uses these questions, illustrations, tables, and graphs the next time when visiting a clinic. If the visit is only for 60 minutes, see how much you can answer. If the visit lasts for three days and the clinic will even provide data, see how much more you can answer.

After visiting one clinic, go see another and repeat the process. Record what you find and reference it even after the process becomes second nature. After repeating the process over and over, the reader will have even more knowledge to add on to what I already provided.

OVERVIEW ON CLINICS INCLUDING THE PEOPLE AND PAYERS

II

Chapter 3

General Questions to Help Understand a Clinic or Medical Practice

Figure 3.1   Summarizes the four general staff groups that collectively work together to provide patient care in clinics.

Who are the Providers?

Provider is an established qualification and role that can diagnose, decide on a plan of care, treat, and bill for services. Providers for a medical practice or simple clinics are typically your physicians – Doctor of Medicine (MD) or Doctor of Osteopathic Medicine (DO), Advanced Practice Registered Nurses – Certified Nurse Practitioner (APRN-CNP) or Certified Nurse Midwife (APRN-CNM), and Physician Assistant (PA). Depending on the state regulations, choice of practice leaders, choice of the system that owns the practice, or the geographic and demographic area, you may find more APRN-CNPs and PAs managing care for their own designated set of patients, rather than extending the services of a physician.

If the clinic is an Orthopedic practice, then expect the providers to be Orthopedic specialists; if it is a Cardiology clinic, expect cardiologists. If the clinic is Primary Care, then there can be Family Medicine, Pediatric, Internal Medicine, and similar provider specialties. As Primary Care continues to include more total care, expect to find psychologists, obstetrics-gynecological, nutritionists, chiropractic, and other total care providers. More and more clinics are becoming "multi-specialty" which simply means providers from different specialties, sometimes complimentary while sometimes not, work in the same clinic and space.

While there are plenty of attributes to understand and characterize a clinic by, knowing the specialty of the clinic providers and composition of providers in large part explains the behavior of the clinic. Different specialties have different processes, different equipment, different paces, and different capacity. For example, surgical specialists like Orthopedics, General Surgery, or Gastroenterology may only spend two full or half days in the actual clinic with the remainder of the days working in an Ambulatory Surgery center, main operating room, or managing inpatient consults at the hospital. While the clinic is important to these providers, the bulk work they provide is not done in the clinic. Cardiologists, Pulmonologists, and other medical specialists may split time outside the clinic providing inpatient consults, performing treatments, or doing procedures, but within the clinic, there may be special diagnostics, treatments, or procedures completed with each patient visit or in addition to a patient visit unique to that specialty.

Who are the Managers and Administrators?

In small clinics or practices, the practice manager is generally charged with managing the day to day of the operations like scheduling, billing, ordering supplies, managing vendors and profit/loss for the clinic while providers and physician leaders provide care. If the organization is physician owned, then typically the physician with the highest stake in the organization is the lead, while more equally distributed ownership may mean that there is no real physician lead or there is an elected physician Lead.

Typically, if the clinic is owned by a larger group or healthcare system, then there is likely some form of a hierarchy like regionalized managers above the practice manager and regionalized physician leaders over the physician practice leader. Instead of a regionalized hierarchy, the hierarchy could be based on the practice specialty or overall service line the specialty is a part of. Generally, the larger the organization is, the more layers there tend to be in the hierarchy.

For larger and busier clinics, there may be a sub-division of leadership under the practice manager that may include a "front office" lead and "back office" Lead. The "front office" is where the administrative functions of the clinic take place like registration, scheduling, billing, medical records, and more. The "back office" is the clinical operation of the clinic that involves the collection of height/weight data, performing lab testing, performing patient exams, completing electronic documentation, ensuring medication management, and more.

Who are the Clinical Staff?

The clinical staff support the providers in the "back office" or remotely. Frequently medical assistants (CMA or MA) are employed to manage a bulk of the non-provider care tasks, but there are also Licensed Practical Nurses/Licensed Vocational Nurses (LPN/LVN), Registered Nurses (RN), and other specialty assistants.

Clinical staff are focused on managing the patient care processes and tasks for each patient that schedules an appointment, arrives at the clinic, or contacts the clinic with clinical questions or concerns, and clinical staff are focused on maintaining engagement with a set of patients between care visits. In many specialties and Primary Care, more often than not, a medical assistant will perform bulk work for patient care while an RN may perform follow-up checks, coordinate care for patients, and assist in procedures. In some clinics there may only be medical assistants while in others LPN/LVNs or RNs are heavily used. The composition and responsibilities of clinical staff often differ by practice specialty, state licensure, and local cultural preferences.

Who are the Support Staff?

The support staff take on the healthcare administrative burden so that clinical staff and providers do not have to take on any or as much of the administrative work. The support staff complete the administrative, financial, technical, and logistical tasks for the clinic. The in-clinic support staff are the "front office" staff that are in the clinic day to day checking patients in for a visit, answering outside phone calls, scanning old paper charts, verifying bills, and more.

Besides the in-clinic support staff, there can be numerous outside entities that support the clinic like Information Technology (IT) support for the electronic medical records, Security for cameras or building alarms, Supply Chain for routine medical supplies, Building Maintenance for managing heating, ventilation, and air conditioning (HVAC) systems, Equipment Maintenance for maintaining diagnostic equipment, and more. For many smaller clinics, these outside support entities are often contracted vendors. For clinics that are part of larger groups or healthcare systems, there is usually a highly variable mix of which support services are managed through the system versus contracted out, though often the contracts are managed by the system with less pushed down to the individual practice manager.

Who are the Patients?

Patients are not all the same as they have different health needs and wants. Patients are different ages and come from different generations; patients come from different income levels; patients have different lifestyles and risk factors; and patients have various preferences. To say the least, there are many ways to segment or classify the various types of patients.

Some clinics take an approach of caring for any patient that can walk through the doors, while other clinics proactively target certain patient groups and segments or, through a charter, serve specific patient groups. For example, a high-end boutique clinic may target those people with high disposable income; a Family Medicine practice may truly target and see families in family visits; an Internal Medicine clinic may target baby boomers; a health center clinic acts as the safety net for the surrounding community; while some other clinic may choose to see all these patient types. Some minds in healthcare are beginning to believe the notion that "you can't be all things to everyone" and believe it is more effective and efficient to manage the care of a specific patient group. This type of thinking has existed for decades in industrial, retail, and other commercial sectors. The belief is that with a more homogenous group of patients, clinics can create a more tailored experience and yet simpler processes to deliver that care experience.

How is the Organization Paid?

How an individual is incentivized at work can explain a great deal about an individual's behavior. Likewise, how a group of individuals is incentivized can explain a great deal about group behavior, processes, and operating practices. In Outpatient Care, there are four general categories for how clinics get paid or receive funding, that is if the clinic gets funded for care.

First, some clinics get reimbursed for every patient visit, which is often called Fee for Service (FFS) or sometimes even transactional medicine. In this model, providers are paid for each encounter with the patient or paid for the work done per patient visit. In healthcare business, it is important that each clinic and provider sees as many if not more patients every day

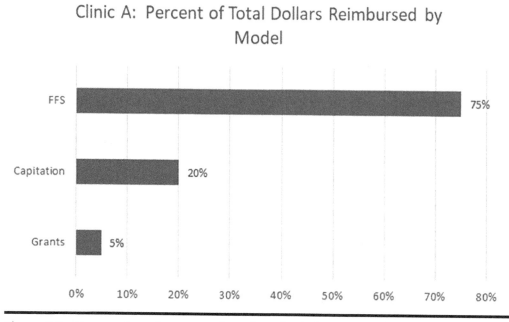

Figure 3.2 **Summarizes the proportion of total reimbursement dollars for Clinic A by each type of patient care reimbursement model that reimburses the clinic. In Clinic A's case, most of the revenue comes from Fee for Service with some capitated reimbursement and a little money from grants for special programs to the community.**

than are accounted for in planned numbers or a visit capacity target. Most payers still use this model of reimbursement to clinics for services rendered.

A challenge with this model is that there is likely a volume of care completed that is not necessary or not as efficient compared to if that volume of care was managed another way. If a provider is incentivized only on seeing patients physically in office visits, then it is less likely a provider will voluntarily conduct frequent telehealth visits, complete EMR e-visits, or have staff complete the follow-up checks.

In addition to the FFS there are often quality or value-based programs attached depending on the payer. The quality programs usually monitor a set of quality measures and base payment reductions or bonuses on how the quality measures perform over a set time period. Usually the payment adjustment is applied to visit payments – an Office Visit of $90 is adjusted down to $85 for a poorer performing clinic while the $90 is increased to $95 for a better performer.

Second, some clinics get funding or a share of funding for every patient that is cared for by the clinic. In this capitated payment model, providers are paid a flat rate per patient that may be paid monthly or annually – Per Member Per Month (PMPM) or Per Member Per Year (PMPY). The payment model is not really that different to a gym membership. Usually this payment model is associated with both Acute and Ambulatory Care working together to make sure the total amount of patient care per patient is appropriate, though this model of reimbursement is also used by Direct Primary Care clinics. In the shared Acute and Ambulatory Care model, the more care a patient consumes and the costlier the care a patient consumes, the less profit there is per patient – there may even be a loss. Often the focus of these programs is to keep patient members out of the Emergency Department or prevent them from being frequently admitted to the Hospital.

Because there is no financial incentive for each patient visit or the total number of visits, the clinic and each provider focuses continuous care on a set number of patients or patient members. The traditional office visit is not the one tool for care delivery. During a traditional office visit, providers can spend more time with each patient to direct them down a wellness path. Providers and teammates can often leverage email, text, and video conference sessions to complete care. A provider's teammates like RNs can take on more care tasks like counseling, follow-up checks, and outreach.

As with Fee for Service, a quality or value-based program can be attached that increases or decreases the overall funding to the clinic. Like the FFS programs, the quality programs usually monitor a set of quality measures and base payment reductions or bonuses on how the quality measures perform over a set time period. Usually the payment adjustment is applied to the PMPM or PMPY reimbursements.

Third, some clinics, especially government types, receive funding through an annual budget allocation or through grant funds to manage as much care as possible with those funds, though the funds are budgeted generally for an expected amount of care per year. There is less focus on the number of visits, or the number of patients managed and more attention to whether the funds cover all the care expenses and whether the funds will increase, decrease, or remain in the next year. Efficiency is a key to success for these clinics as well as often managing years of operation with few large capital allotments for major infrastructure work or equipment purchase.

Organizations that run completely on fixed budgets and grant funding face challenges when patient demands vary from expectations. For instance, if patient demands for a clinic far exceed what was expected, then that clinic may not have the funds to purchase enough supplies or pay extended hours for staff labor. Likewise, if the budget funding or grant funds shrink while patient demands remain constant, then a clinic may no longer have enough funds to purchase enough supplies or pay extended hours for staff labor. On the other hand, just because patient demands decrease, many clinics' funding does not shrink, though it possibly could.

Four, many clinics are faced with juggling multiple reimbursement models as well as not receiving reimbursement from some patients. Many traditional clinics have a strong foundation in Fee for Service, but as population health models become more common, a portion of care has shifted to a capitated payment scheme. Depending on clinic services and programs, a share of patient care services may also be funded through grants.

A new reality and challenge is that a clinic may have 50% of patients in old FFS programs and 50% in newer capitated plans. These organizations face a challenge of whether to treat patients differently based on each patient's reimbursement plan, which may increase process complexity, or whether to treat patients all the same so processes are simplified, though there could be less optimal reimbursement.

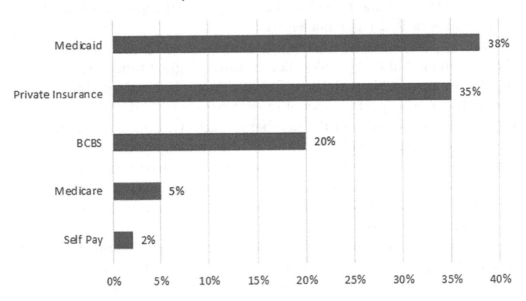

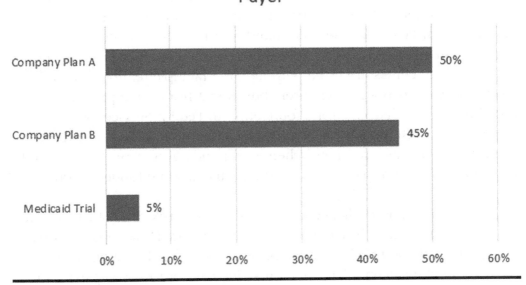

Figure 3.3 Summarizes the proportion of total reimbursement for each reimbursement model for Clinic A by each Payer. The FFS revenue is coming from five main sources 1) Medicaid 2) Private Insurance 3) Blue Cross Blue Shield 4) Medicare and 5) Self payers. The capitated revenue is coming from three main sources 1) a local business (Plan A) that pays the clinic a PMPM fee 2) another local business (Plan B) that pays the clinic a PMPM fee and 3) a new Medicaid capitated model trial.

What is the Payer Mix?

In healthcare there are many payers such as Blue Cross Blue Shield, Medicare, Medicaid, Private Insurance, Self-Pay, or even No Pay. Each payer may have several plans that pay differently for the same care or pay different PMPM rates for managing members. Each payer may offer a capitated reimbursement program or Fee for Service. The payer mix describes the proportions of each payer and plan, and sums up the "typical" reimbursement per visit or "typical" PMPM payment.

Organizations with a favorable or healthy payer mix tend to get a more generous reimbursement or larger PMPM payments, which make it easier to manage the bottom line as long as the organization has enough patient visit volumes or patient members while the clinic controls excess costs. Organizations with a higher proportion of patients with private insurance tend to have a healthier payer mix as long as the negotiated reimbursements are comfortable. Organizations with less favorable payer mixes get lower reimbursements which makes managing the bottom line a feat in controlling costs, running lean, and using scale. Organizations with a less favorable payer mix generally have more Medicaid patients.

PATIENT THROUGHPUT, PATIENT FLOW, AND CAPACITY

Chapter 4

Questions to Understand How Patients Access Care or Patient Access

What Type of Care do Patients Access?

The first component of patient access is knowing the types of care that a patient is accessing or what types they need. Patients might seek a Same

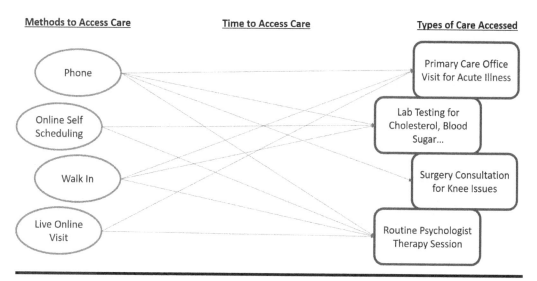

Figure 4.1   Shows three components to how patients access care: 1) the types of services accessed 2) the method patients use to access the patient care services and 3) the time it takes to receive the patient care services upon accessing.

Day medical appointment for an acute reason such as flu-like symptoms. A patient might seek an Annual Wellness check for next year. A patient might need a follow-up visit after being discharged from a hospital. A patient may need chronic condition management. A patient might need nutrition education to help reduce risks of heart conditions. There are many different types of needs, wants, and services to access. The type of care patients access from a clinic is of course related to the type of specialties the providers practice and to a degree the type of reimbursement model, but each clinic may have differences to note.

Additionally, clinics may offer a variety of diagnostic testing within the clinic such as lab tests – urinalysis, CBC, Strep test, flu testing or imaging services – chest X-ray, CT of the abdomen, or ultrasound. Often diagnostic testing services done within a clinic are those most frequently ordered by the providers which means patients do not have to travel to another site for this testing. It also means that providers can usually get feedback faster and, for the clinic, it serves as a complimentary source of revenue.

Deciding and defining the care services a clinic or organization offers is a balance between patient demands, patient convenience, provider convenience, and profitability of the services. Clinics of different scales, in different markets, within different organizational structures, and of different specialties will come to different conclusions on what services are offered at the clinic.

How do Patients Access Care?

The second component to patient access is physically the method of how patients access the care that is available or the care that they need. Two high level categories of accessing care are a) spontaneously arriving or b) scheduling to arrive. From these two high level categories there are many different options and specific clinics will offer many of these options or may just offer one option to access care.

Spontaneous Arrival: Without teleportation, patients tend not to just appear; however, patients can physically walk into a clinic unannounced without an appointment and seek care. Through technology modes, patients can instantly access teleconference visits without pre-scheduling. An often undervalued type of care is when patients just have care questions or need help deciding on a course of action. Patients will spontaneously ask questions through email, text-style messages with the provider, or walk-in.

Because spontaneous care is not planned, the response time to receive care often depends on how many other patients have priority, or there might be an overall lack of resources, or maybe just a lack at that specific time.

Spontaneous care can be challenging to manage because of the uncertainty of when and how many patients arrive. Day by day and hour by hour, there can be rushes of patients that temporarily exceed the care team's capacity to treat in a timely manner and there can be complete lull periods with no patients, all in the same day. Usually, when reviewing patient arrival data over a long time period, trends emerge that can indicate how best to match capacity to demand, but even this does not prevent backups or lulls. Managing clinics with spontaneous services is usually an investment in best fitting coverage. Coverage is designed to satisfy the demands of a specific patient segment that wants the convenience of walk-in or being able to access care when access is needed without much delay.

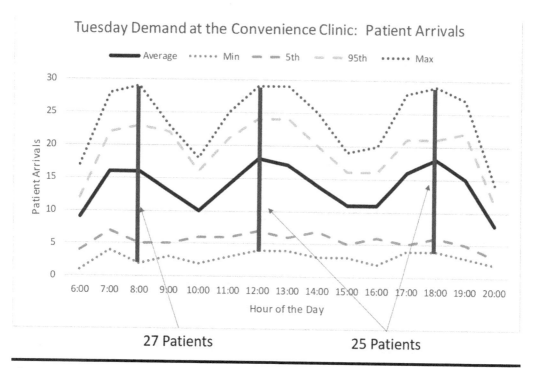

Figure 4.2 Illustrates the variability in how patients may arrive at a walk-in clinic. The above chart graphs the number of patients that arrive at a convenient walk-in clinic by hour of the day. The graph highlights the average number of patient arrivals as well as the peaks (95th percentile and Max) and lulls (5th percentile and Min). At 8am there have been as few as two patients arriving but there have also been 29 patients arriving or a range of 27 patients to prepare for.

Scheduled Arrival: More clinics tend to have the basic "schedule an appointment" method to accessing care. There are many modes to scheduling an appointment which include picking up a phone and calling, electronically allowing patients to self-schedule a specific appointment time, electronically allowing patients to request an appointment, and more. Clinics that deploy scheduled patient care do it to get a consistent productivity level out of providers, create stability in the clinic, and simply provide pre-planned time for patients to meet with providers – after all, not all care needs are urgent.

Managing scheduled clinics can be challenging because not every patient wants to wait for an appointment, not all appointment times or dates meet patient needs, not all care needs can be scheduled the "right" amount of time, and some patients have care priorities that need more attention or need to be seen sooner. Typical struggles with scheduled care occur when patients do not show up, patients do not show up on time, providers run behind, or providers have to rebook entire groups of patients due to unforeseen conflicts with their own schedule.

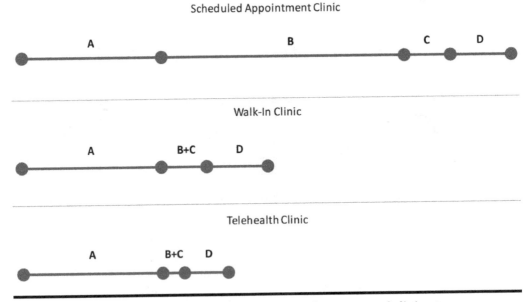

Figure 4.3 Shows the timeline to access care for three types of clinics (one scheduled to arrive clinic and two spontaneous arrival clinics). A) is the pre-engagement period where a patient self-assesses and decides whether or not to seek care B) is the steps and time to access care C) is the time waiting once care has been accessed and D) is the patient care service time. For walk-in and telehealth clinics, B and C are together because accessing and waiting for care to begin occur at roughly the same time.

Mixed Methods: Many clinics operate with the capability to manage both spontaneous and scheduled patients. A clinic might schedule follow-up appointments or non-urgent appointments in advance because that is a patient preference, while maintaining flexibility in the day to accommodate patients with Same Day urgent needs.

How Long do Patients Wait to Access Care?

Measuring how long it takes to get access to care is a key performance measure for clinics because it helps identify the availability of clinical services and potential capacity deficiencies of those services for a given clinic. Further, the wait time to access care can often dwarf any wait time a patient faces once they physically arrive at a clinic for care, so it is a good accompanying measure for patient satisfaction or dissatisfaction.

One way to measure Patient Access times is by retrospectively assessing the lead time from when a patient requests services to when the patient receives the services. The patient request for services might be the date and time a patient calls to make an appointment, the time the patient walks in the door for urgent care, or the date and time the patient sends a secure care text message to a provider.

In a walk-in clinic, the lead time to access care is roughly the same time a patient spends waiting in the clinic and is more likely to be measured as patient wait time. In a scheduled clinic, Patient Access accounts for the days it takes to get into the clinic before the wait time once inside the clinic begins. Usually the wait time in the clinic is minutes or hours compared to the days it takes to get into a clinic. For this reason, Patient Access is often measured in days from zero on up.

Another way to look ahead to measure Patient Access is by identifying the likely date and time a patient will receive care if that patient requested services now. In walk-in clinics, this is calculated as an expected wait time rather than Patient Access and it is based on the number of patients ahead in line combined with the typical amount of time the provider spends per patient. In a scheduled clinic, the measure is calculated on the number of days from today until the next appointment is available. More common, and often preferred by users, is understanding the number of days out until the third next open time slot is available. The third next available appointment availability is thought to exclude unwanted or less desirable appointment slots though the slots are still open times on a provider's schedule.

Patient ID	Type of Appointment	Provider Name	Date Appointment was made	Date Appointment was Completed	Lead Time
zzzzz1111	New	D. Jones	10/1/2018	10/8/2018	7
zzzzz1112	New	D. Jones	10/1/2018	10/31/2018	30
zzzzz1113	New	D. Jones	10/2/2018	10/12/2018	10
zzzzz1114	New	D. Jones	10/2/2018	10/30/2018	28
zzzzz1115	New	D. Jones	10/4/2018	10/16/2018	12
zzzzz1116	New	D. Jones	10/4/2018	11/2/2018	29
zzzzz1117	New	D. Jones	10/5/2018	10/25/2018	20
zzzzz1118	New	D. Jones	10/8/2018	10/12/2018	4
zzzzz1119	New	D. Jones	10/9/2018	10/22/2018	13
zzzzz1120	New	D. Jones	10/9/2018	11/2/2018	24
zzzzz1121	New	D. Jones	10/10/2018	10/19/2018	9
zzzzz1122	New	D. Jones	10/10/2018	10/26/2018	16
zzzzz1123	New	D. Jones	10/11/2018	10/19/2018	8
zzzzz1124	New	D. Jones	10/12/2018	10/22/2018	10
				Average Lead Time (days)	15.7

Continued

Figure 4.4 Shows a table with the appointment information needed to calculate lead time in days for New Patient Appointments seeing Dr. D. Jones. The data can be extracted from the EMR, scheduling system or manually transcribed from records.

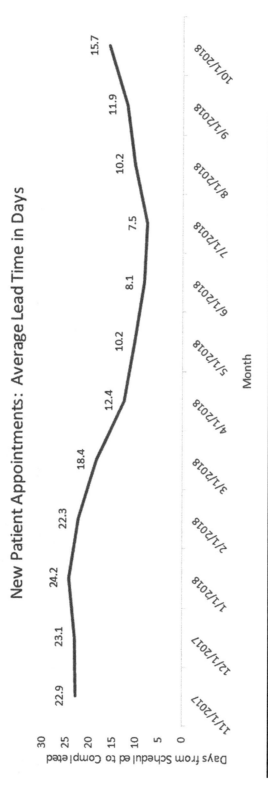

Figure 4.5 Shows trending of the average monthly lead time by month for New Patient Appointments seeing Dr. D. Jones. A time series line chart helps pick up on trends and seasonal affects, and is helpful to compare against goals.

Date of Measurement	Appointment Type	Provider Name	Date for Third Next Available Appointment	Days Out
10/1/2018	New Patient	D. Jones	10/15/2018	14
10/2/2018	New Patient	D. Jones	10/17/2018	15
10/3/2018	New Patient	D. Jones	10/22/2018	19
10/4/2018	New Patient	D. Jones	10/12/2018	8
10/5/2018	New Patient	D. Jones	10/22/2018	17
10/8/2018	New Patient	D. Jones	10/23/2018	15
10/9/2018	New Patient	D. Jones	10/24/2018	15
10/10/2018	New Patient	D. Jones	10/22/2018	12
10/11/2018	New Patient	D. Jones	10/26/2018	15
10/12/2018	New Patient	D. Jones	10/30/2018	18
		Continued		
			Average days out in days	14.8

Figure 4.6 Shows a table with the appointment information needed to calculate days until the third next available appointment New Patient Appointments seeing Dr. D. Jones. The data can be automatically processed in some scheduling systems or may be manually audited. For example, "Date of Measurement" is the audit date where an administrator looks forward to identify the date of the third next available appointment.

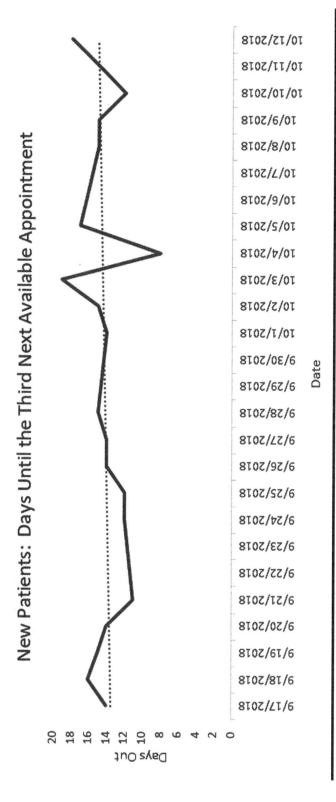

Figure 4.7 Shows trending of days until the third next available appointment by date for New Patient Appointments seeing Dr. D. Jones. A time series line chart helps pick up on trends, can project future performance, and compare to desired goals.

For clinics that have specific appointment slots for designated services, when measuring and reporting on patient access, it is important to measure the overall average number of days until the third next available appointment for each slot – Same Day appointments, specific New Patient appointments, Annual Wellness appointments, and monthly follow-ups. There is value in knowing the patient access days for each specific appointment type. For example, if Same Day appointments are not available for the next four days or New Patient appointments are not available until three months out, then there may be capacity or scheduling issues to mitigate.

For clinics that do not have specific appointment slots for designated services, one will measure simply the third next available slot no matter what the reason for the patient visit. Many clinics that strive for patient accommodation or use open access style schedules will have only one measure for third next available appointments as opposed to one for each appointment type.

Chapter 5

Questions to Understand the Basics of the Clinic Capacity

What Types of Point of Care Space Exist?

Point of care space is the specific location in a clinic where value added care is provided to a patient by a caregiver. Examples of point of care space in clinics are the exam rooms, procedure rooms, phlebotomy or blood draw stations, the scale to collect height and weight if it is outside the exam room, a private telehealth or teleconference computer station, and other diagnostic space. Point of care space is not the administrative space, the waiting room, staff breakrooms, hallways, or offices. The point of care space is simply where the true care is provided.

Point of care space is often associated with a specific care service, for instance a blood draw station is for the lab. Other point of care space is planned to be more flexible like an exam room that provides exam space for a variety of physician specialties, minor procedure space for those physicians, and even education or nutritional counseling space. Knowing the composition of what point of care locations exist can help identify the simplicity or complexity of a given clinic and how flexible the clinic space is for which care providers.

How Many Point of Care Spaces Exist?

After knowing what types of point of care space exist, find out how many of each type of space exist. The number of point of care locations will indicate the number of providers and caregivers that can operate in the same clinic at

Type of Spcae	Specific Space	Quantity	Comments
Point of Care Space	Exam Rooms	36	All multi use Exam Rooms
Point of Care Space	Lab/Collection	2	Blood draw stations
Point of Care Space	X-Ray Room	1	None
Point of Care Space	CT Room	1	None
Point of Care Space	Psychologist Room	1	None
Point of Care Space	Physical Therapy Area	1	Up to 8 patients simultaneously
	Total	42	

Figure 5.1 Shows a quick inventory of all point of care space in a clinic. A simple inventory can be expanded to include square footage of the point of care space and non-point of care space too.

the same time. The amount of point of care space is one of the overall clinic capacity limiters. For example, a Family Medicine clinic with 15 exam rooms has more potential capacity to see patients than a Family Medicine clinic with 12 exam rooms, while another clinic with 36 exam rooms, two procedure rooms, two lab draw stations, one CT room, and one X-ray has even more potential capacity. Keep in mind that this capacity is all just potential.

What Hours of the Day and Days of the Week is the Clinic Open?

Just because a clinic has a great deal of potential capacity for patient care, does not mean that the capacity is realized. A neighborhood restaurant, a nearby supermarket, or corner gas station, all are businesses that decide on which hours of which days to open. A clinic is open or closed in the same way and clinic leadership makes the decision on which hours to open or close in order to best satisfy patient demands while managing costs.

Rarely are clinics open 24/7/365. Many traditional clinics are open Monday–Friday during common business hours of 8am–5pm which translates to 45 hours out of 168 hours per week, or being open roughly 27% of the week. Other clinics are open other hours or more hours each week, often in hopes of improving patients' access to care or better managing a large patient demand. Some clinics have holiday and weekend hours while others remain closed.

In some clinics, the hours of operation will vary for each service. For example, lab draw services may be open from 6am–6pm, X-ray may be open from 7pm–4pm, and the exam clinic is open 8am–5pm.

How Many Providers are Working During Which Hours and Days?

In addition to knowing which hours and days of the week a clinic is open, to understand capacity of a clinic, it is important to know the number of providers that are seeing patients over which times and days. Providers are normal people with families and lives outside the clinic. While a clinic is open, not all providers start seeing patients at the same time, work the same days, work the same number of hours, or leave at the same time.

Weekly Hours of Operation per Service (Hours Seeing Patients)

Service Name	Monday			Tuesday			Wednesday			Thursday			Friday		
	Start	End	Total	Start	End	Total	Start	End	Total	Start	End	Total	Start	End	Total
Office Visits	7:00	18:00	11	8:00	17:00	9	8:00	17:00	9	8:00	17:00	9	8:00	19:00	11
Lab	7:00	18:00	11	7:00	18:00	11	7:00	18:00	11	7:00	18:00	11	7:00	18:00	11
Imaging	7:00	18:00	11	7:00	18:00	11	8:00	17:00	9	8:00	17:00	9	8:00	17:00	9

Total Hours	Hours Available	% Open
49	168	29.2%
55	168	32.7%
49	168	29.2%

Figure 5.2 Shows the hours of operation for three patient care services in one clinic. Lab is open the most in a week at 55 hours while both imaging and office visits are open 49 hours a week though open at different hours on some days of the week. The clinic is not open on weekends and, except Fridays, not open past 6pm. No service is open more than 1/3 of the available 168 hours in a week.

Weekly Provider Schedule and Total Hours Scheduled (Less 1 Hour for Lunch)

Provider Name	Monday Start	Monday End	Monday Total	Tuesday Start	Tuesday End	Tuesday Total	Wednesday Start	Wednesday End	Wednesday Total	Thursday Start	Thursday End	Thursday Total	Friday Start	Friday End	Friday Total	Total
D. Jones	8:00	17:00	8	8:00	12:00	4	8:00	17:00	8	8:00	17:00	8	8:00	17:00	8	36
J. Doe	8:30	17:30	8	8:30	17:30	8	8:30	15:30	6	8:30	15:30	6	8:30	17:30	8	36
W. Smith	7:30	16:30	8	7:30	16:30	8	7:30	16:30	8	7:30	11:30	4	7:30	16:30	8	36
A. Thomas	7:30	16:30	8	7:30	16:30	8	7:30	16:30	8	7:30	16:30	8			0	32
L. King	8:00	17:00	8	8:00	17:00	8	8:00	12:00	4	8:00	17:00	8	8:00	17:00	8	36
Total			40			36			34			34			32	176

Figure 5.3 Shows that there are five providers who work in the clinic. Four providers devote 36 hours a week to scheduled patient care (though the providers may spend many more hours outside of the 36 in patient care related activities) and one provider devotes 32 hours a week. Overall, the five providers devote 176 hours a week to direct patient care or care capacity though the number of hours vary each day of the week.

Annual Provider Hours	
Provider Name	Total Hours
D. Jones	1,728
J. Doe	1,584
W. Smith	1,440
A. Thomas	1,440
L. King	1,512
Total	7,704

Figure 5.4 **Shows the annual hours scheduled for patient care for the same five providers listed in Figure 5.3. While four of the five have the same weekly schedule, the four each have a very different number of hours over the course of the year.**

Providers might also work a very different number of hours over a year because some might work part-time, some might work full-time, some take more holidays, and full-time for some may actually be more hours than others that work full-time. Work contracts and expectations can be very different for providers in an organization and within the same clinic.

Provider hours is another one of the key capacity limiters for a clinic. Learning the hours for a clinic will help identify a planned operational capacity for that clinic which further can be compared to the clinic's actual performance against that planned capacity.

How Many Providers are Working Compared to Space Available to Work?

Clinic visits can be very quick or take up to an hour, it really depends on the provider, specialty, and reason for the visit. Exam rooms in clinics are a resource used by providers and ideally there are enough rooms for each provider so as to not slow down a provider's work pace. After understanding when providers work and how those hours may vary, it is helpful to match that information to the number of point of care locations in the clinic available for each provider to use.

Clinic Session	Exam Rooms Available	Providers Working	Rooms per Provider
Monday AM	24	12	2.0
Monday PM	24	12	2.0
Tuesday AM	24	10	2.4
Tuesday PM	24	10	2.4
Wednesday AM	24	9	2.7
Wednesday PM	24	8	3.0
Thursday AM	24	10	2.4
Thursday PM	24	8	3.0
Friday AM	24	7	3.4
Friday PM	24	7	3.4

Figure 5.5   Compares the number of exam rooms counted from the room inventory to the number of providers scheduled to work each session and day of the week. The rooms per provider fluctuate throughout the week and can be not enough for optimal throughput or surplus space.

Provider productivity may suffer if a provider does not have enough rooms in which to work efficiently, especially those providers that see patients at a faster pace. At some point having more rooms no longer increases workflow efficiency and becomes inefficient for the whole clinic. There is a loss of potential throughput for other providers that can work in the clinic because rooms are consumed by a provider that is using more rooms than needed. Thus there is a loss to potential clinic capacity. Learning at which times and days room allocations may actually hinder efficiency or lose potential capacity can help shift resources to create more output.

Chapter 6

Questions to Understand what Happens before the Patient Visits

How Much of the Check-In, Registration, and Payment Processing can a Patient do Before Setting Foot in the Clinic?

As technology adoption expands, more administrative tasks normally done at the check-in desk are completed before a patient arrives, thus freeing up patient and resource time in the clinic. Realistically, the idea of healthcare pre-check or pre-registration processes is not so different to online airplane flight check-in processes or even online movie reservation processes. Typically, this service pre-check-in offering is seen as a positive for many patients especially more technology savvy patients, patients seeking convenience, and patients seeking efficiency.

Via online portals, patients can update insurance, maintain an updated address and contact information. Patients can electronically sign HIPAA and Consent to Treat forms. In some cases, a co-payment might be pre-paid or payment information started which reduces the work cycle time in the clinic.

In some clinics there may nothing done ahead of the visit other than potentially collecting some information over the phone at the time of scheduling, and in many cases there is nothing wrong with the process because the process best serves certain types of patients. Having learned about the type of pre-check-in capabilities a clinic has, it is important to

In Clinic Traditional Patient Check In Time Compared to Online Pre-Check			
Process Step	**Traditional**	**Online Pre-Check**	
		Remote	**In Clinic**
Shows Identification and Identifier at Check In	0.5		0.5
Updates Insurance and Contact Information	0.5	0.5	
Signs Consent to Treat and HIPAA Forms	1	1	
Pays the Co-Pay	1	1	
Updates History and Health Screening Forms	5	5	
Total	**8**	**7.5**	**0.5**

Figure 6.1   Compares a traditional patient Check-in process in the clinic to one where much of the work is completed remotely by the patient. In this case, the patient has to spend about 7.5 fewer minutes completing Check-in tasks in the clinic while the front desk staff save a couple minutes per Check-in and likely have fewer disruptions.

review whether the process is more efficient and more appropriate for the intended patients. After all, not all patients are looking for technology savvy efficiencies and not all online process are efficient enough to satisfy patients.

How Much Health Screening and Form Filling Out is Done in Advance?

There is a great deal of information needed from each patient or family member to give the care team an understanding of a patient's health. Much of this information is collected manually from a patient who fills out forms. The bulk of information is collected on the very first visit for a New Patient, including thorough medical histories, but patients having an Annual Wellness visit may be asked to update annual health goals, while all patients may be asked to update current medications.

Rather than patients filling out several forms on a clipboard after arriving at the clinic, some organizations push that information to the patient electronically via a patient portal, while some may simply mail forms to the patient weeks in advance. From an efficiency standpoint, electronically collected information saves time once a patient sets foot inside the clinic and if the electronic forms are integrated into the medical records, then that information can automatically update for the specific visit notes, thus saving staff time in transcription. At the same time, clunky online questionnaires might never be completed by a patient before a visit and clunky software might make online forms digitally less useful than paper forms to providers and staff. After learning about the type of online form filling capabilities a clinic has, it is important to review whether the process is more efficient and more appropriate for the intended patients just like pre-check processes.

What Tasks do the Front Office do to Prepare for Each Patient that Visits?

Rather than wait till the time a patient shows up at the Front Desk, many clinics complete work ahead of time so that the patient and provider do not have to wait once the patient arrives. Often, there is a checklist associated with the items a front desk staff member reviews for each patient and sometimes that checklist is completed within the electronic health record system or something like it. The front desk staff may need to make sure a patient has paid for all previous services, may need to update insurance, and may need to collect outside health records to imbed in the patient health record. Knowing what work is prepared ahead of time is a good indicator for how proactive and efficient a clinic is once patients arrive.

What Tasks do the Clinical Staff do to Prepare for Each Patient that Visits?

Much like the front office staff, the clinical staff may prepare for each patient ahead of time rather than wait till the time a patient shows up at the front desk. Typical preparation tasks that staff may do for a specific patient are: preparing lab collection supplies for urinalysis, preparing minor procedure supplies for a pap smear, verifying all outside records have been added to the patient record, color coding each patient chart or electronic tracker to indicate what a specific patient will need in that visit, and more. Again, the work prepared ahead of time is a good indicator for how proactive and efficient a clinic is once patients arrive.

What Tasks do Providers do to Prepare for Each Patient that Visits?

Providers will often prepare ahead as well for each patient visit. Providers will often review the last visit note the patient had with the provider and review any outside test results or notes from another provider. Providers may do a quick check to understand the mix of all patients coming in the door and communicate with the provider's assigned clinical support team member on what additional items need preparation.

Chapter 7

Questions to Understand Location of a Clinic and a Location Strategy for the Clinic

Physically, Where is the Clinic Located?

Though patients are willing to travel distances for care, outpatient care is still relatively local so where a clinic is located tends to identify the catchment area of the patients the clinic serves. The location of a clinic matters to patients. Depending on which patient segments a clinic serves or targets, location can be advantageous or even seen as a differentiator by patients. For example, a medical practice that focuses on geriatric patients that frequently see multiple providers and get routine tests may benefit more if the clinic is in the same building or near other providers and services that care for the same patients. On the other hand, a general pediatric clinic located on a medical campus that is over a 20-minute commute from the nearest neighborhood where kids live, and requires ten minutes to find a parking spot in a parking garage, may be a less desirable experience for patients. Further, as technology advances, a clinic that is only a minute of Skype or Facetime away might be an extremely convenient location for some patients to receive care.

Much like home real estate markets, commercial locations also face varying costs and prices, so the location of a clinic can further determine some of the overhead costs a clinic faces. Clinics in higher end parts of town or located in newer commercial retail centers might pay a premium for rent compared to those in other parts of town.

Physically What Type of Space is it?

Unless an office visit is completed via phone or electronically, patients will physically enter a building. The type of space can matter to both the patients and the organization. There are a handful of ways to describe a clinic and the space within a clinic. The descriptions below are not mutually exclusive but offer a broad method to categorize clinics.

1. Community Clinic → a community clinic is a smaller "outpost" providing care in a geographic area. The community clinic is the classic small practice clinic in a strip mall or on the corner of the neighborhood. The community clinic is generally small and has a limited number of different services. Community clinics are good buildings for small practices or primary care groups to increase access points for patients or an option for organizations that choose to enter into new markets.

2. Multi-Tenant → a multi-tenant clinic is a larger medical office building that houses multiple clinics, practices, or care services and is often called a Medical Office Building or MOB. Typically, the tenants of the building lease the space and often do not work or integrate with the other tenants in the same building on patient care. Each tenant manages its own clinic to include front office services. A simple way to view a multi-tenant building is a building that fits multiple community clinics in one space or is the apartment building for clinics. Multi-tenant buildings can be a good option for an organization to house different specialty services that do not routinely work with other services because the building itself can become a focal location for an organization's disparate specialty services.

3. Multi-specialty → a multi-specialty clinic is like a multi-tenant clinic in that it houses multiple specialties. The difference is that the specialties in the multi-specialty clinic tend to work together routinely on patient care, often in sequence, and share administrative or front office resources. In a multi-specialty clinic, a patient might check-in at any number of check-in stations but usually only needs to check-in once and then may proceed to one or more visits or treatments in the same building. Multi-specialty

clinics tend to be more administratively efficient for an organization and also offer fewer administrative stops for patients that have multiple visits in one day.

4. Multi-Purpose → a multi-purpose clinic is a clinic that shares to accommodate a variety of different providers and clinical services. The shared space means that completely different specialty providers and clinical support staff are seeing patients one day or hour in a space; the next day another provider of a different specialty will see patients in that same space. Multi-purpose space exists so providers or practices do not own space and an organization can get the most out of the physical space it has available. Multi-purpose space also allows certain providers, especially Specialists, to circulate through different clinics throughout a week or month to see patients in other geographic regions.

5. Ambulatory Care center → an Ambulatory Care center may be called a clinic but in reality is more of an outpatient version of a hospital. The Ambulatory Care center tends to have Urgent Care services, Ambulatory Procedure areas, imaging modalities, lab services, therapy services, and clinic space. One section of the Ambulatory Care center may have multi-tenant space for disparate specialty clinics and on the other end may have a multi-specialty clinic. Much like Acute Care medical centers centralize a great many healthcare services into one campus, the Ambulatory Care center does the same for outpatient care.

How Accessible is the Clinic?

Not all patients are able to drive to a clinic and not all clinic visits can be done remotely over email. It is helpful to understand how easy it is for patients to physically get into a clinic whether that is knowing the distance from the bus stop to the clinic, the price and distance from a parking garage, distance from the expressway, how many and how close handicap parking spaces are to the entrance, how many hallways or stories must a patient walk, and more. To a patient, the experience begins once he or she leaves home, work, or from an origin to the clinic visit and then again leaves after the visit. Often this travel experience takes the most time of the whole experience. Often the travel is costly, frustrating or even dangerous.

Another component to accessibility is learning how well the clinic maintains and prepares for patients and staff with disabilities. Electronic doors break, wheelchair ramps get slick, passageways can be too narrow, elevators need repair, and more. If the patient experience for disabled patients is dramatically different and more cumbersome than for a patient without, then an organization has not spent the time thinking through the process or is short of the money to adequately serve all.

What is the Market Competition Like in the Area?

Competition in healthcare is much the same as competition in other industries, especially local retail. In a more crowded competitive market, clinics may try to differentiate themselves in order to retain and attract patients, while in some other regions, there might be no other competitor for 100 miles and a clinic does little to set itself apart or even modernize over the years.

Competition is not all just local any more either. As technology adoption increases, insurance payers, employers, and even health systems are offering more and more remote care to members. Businesses are making agreements nationally with top healthcare providers so that expensive specialty care can be completed by the best in class provider for quality and price even though the care is in a whole other state or city.

Is there a Location Strategy for the Clinic?

Some clinics are in a building because that was the building or land available when the practice began. Other clinics were sited and designed for specific reasons. Building a technology infused community clinic inside a mall or grocery store in a new market may help an organization attract new patients. Consolidating twelve specialty clinics in one multi-tenant clinic may reduce costs and improve efficiency. Swapping the location of a general pediatric practice from a Medical Office Building on a Medical Campus to a neighborhood Community Clinic that housed an Internal Medicine clinic may improve patient satisfaction in both clinics.

There are possibly many reasons for a clinic to be located where it is. Some reasons may be part of a bigger strategy while others are not. It is worth asking, assessing, and understanding the big picture, or even possible gaps in the big picture, whether there was a strategy behind the location or not.

Chapter 8

Questions to Understand how Patients Arrive and Register

How do Patients Find Registration?

Patients may arrive at a clinic by train or bus, on their own two feet, or in a car, but once at the clinic, it may not be easy for the patient to find the clinic registration. Finding registration in a community clinic is usually simple because there is not much to the clinic, but in multi-tenant buildings or larger Ambulatory Care centers navigating to registration may be confusing.

Organizations often deploy signage, zone numbers, color schemes and more creative features to make finding a particular clinic easier. Sometimes finding a clinic and its registration area is easy for patients, while other times it is difficult. The navigation features may be effective or not so effective. If patients find it challenging to locate registration or a clinic, then patient dissatisfaction grows even before checking in with the clinic.

Where and How do Patients Check-in?

The check-in process for clinics is evolving. As mentioned earlier, patients are beginning to complete many check-in and registration steps prior to arriving at a clinic. Once physically inside a clinic, patients often interact with technology in the check-in process. Registration kiosks and mobile devices issued to complete a check-in, form filling, and provide online learning content are common technology items deployed to change patient registration. Sometimes the large traditional check-in desk is set aside for a

Figure 8.1   Shows a traditional Check-in desk. The Check-in desk is situated in a small waiting room and the desk itself separates the front office staff from the patients. In this process there is one member of Check-in staff, as seen by the one computer terminal, though others behind the glass wall could help when needed to speed up the process.

much more open hostess style station that allows a staff member to circulate around the waiting room and kiosks to support patients that are checking in.

Even with the use of technology, many clinics still require some interaction with a staff member, whether that is to show a picture ID to verify identification matched to a picture on record or to fill out a new health screening form that is not digital yet. Technology can often make a registration process more efficient for staff and the patient, but a poorly implemented technology solution can unfortunately make a registration process less efficient and frustrating for the patient.

While check-in seems straight forward, there are many steps involved that may vary by patient because of the reason for the visit, type of appointment, and preference of the patient, as well as the provider seeing the patient and more. Learning each check-in process variant, the efficiency of each process, and the time each step takes will help identify how satisfactory the overall

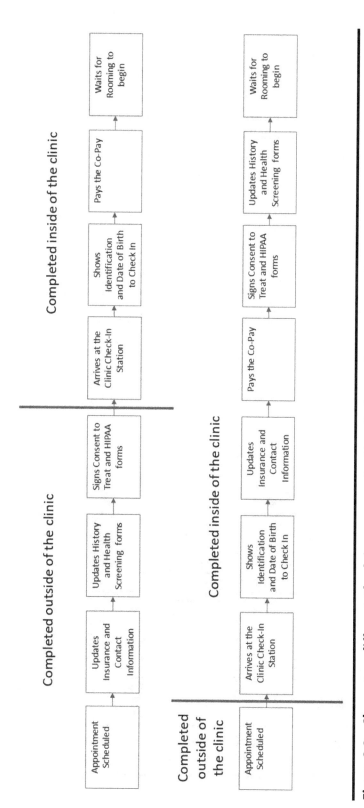

Completed outside of the clinic

Completed inside of the clinic

Appointment Scheduled → Updates Insurance and Contact Information → Updates History and Health Screening forms → Signs Consent to Treat and HIPAA forms → Arrives at the Clinic Check-In Station → Shows Identification and Date of Birth to Check In → Pays the Co-Pay → Waits for Rooming to begin

Completed outside of the clinic

Completed inside of the clinic

Appointment Scheduled → Arrives at the Clinic Check-In Station → Shows Identification and Date of Birth to Check In → Updates Insurance and Contact Information → Pays the Co-Pay → Signs Consent to Treat and HIPAA forms → Updates History and Health Screening forms → Waits for Rooming to begin

Figure 8.2 Shows two different Check-in processes for New Patients. The process at the top uses mobile technology to allow more tasks to be completed outside the clinic at a patient's leisure while the bottom process completes all Check-in tasks inside the clinic.

check-in experience is for a patient. Check-in cycle times should be quick so as to avoid forming a queue. Ideally a check-in should involve only one encounter and not require the patient to come back to the desk multiple times, which can further form a queue. If technology is deployed, then it is important to assess whether the process for both patients and staff is more or equally efficient to what it was without technology. While technology can make registration more efficient for staff, poorly designed technology processes often increase the amount of time patients spend checking in.

Is the Check-in Private?

The check-in process for an appointment might involve answering questions out loud. Discussing payment information or personal information out loud is not comfortable for everyone, especially if another patient is right behind

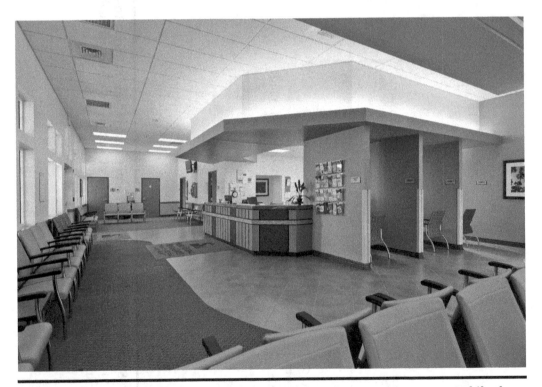

Figure 8.3 Shows a Check-in desk in the middle of a large waiting room. While the Check-in desk is not too far from the entrance vestibule and patient seats, there are three private cut outs (on the right) for private patient interactions or more lengthy patient registrations.

in line or next to them. Some clinics have a very private and personalized check-in experience while other clinics have processes that closely resemble what the Department of Motor Vehicles does.

If the physical space available restricts a clinic's options to provide more privacy at check-in, then the front office staff should deploy less verbal methods to completing registrations privately. For patients, the registration process is the second encounter with staff after scheduling, but usually the first in person. A private and efficient check-in can generate positivity for patients while the opposite process quickly generates patient dissatisfaction.

Does a Line Form and Where Does it Form?

If multiple providers are seeing patients on roughly the same schedule, then it is likely that multiple patients arrive within a similar time window. The

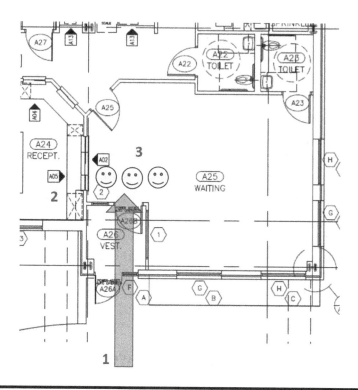

Figure 8.4   Shows a Check-in desk (2) in close proximity to the patient entrance vestibule (1) and the associated line that forms (3) right in front of the vestibule. Even with a relatively empty waiting room, a backup of just a few patients at Check-in that impacts other patients' entrance can create the perception of overcrowding.

rush of patients can be more than the registration staff can handle at once so a line might form even if the check-in process is quick. Depending on how well thought out the entrance and check-in desk is, a line may form back to the entrance doors or vestibule from the registration desk. There may only be a few patients in line for a few minutes, but this backup close to the entrance gives the appearance of a clinic being overwhelmed, backed up, or overcrowded.

Do Patients Check-Out in the Same Spot?

After a patient has seen a provider and is discharged from the clinic, some clinics require patients to go back out to the check-in station. From a patient flow and satisfaction standpoint this is not ideal because arriving patients are vying in line with exiting patients. An exiting patient may have questions on his or her care, need to schedule an appointment, or need files printed, while newly arriving patients are looking for a quick check-in. If the process has patients checking out back at check-in, then volumes at check-in double and realistically a check-out is more time consuming for staff than a check-in. For clinics with multiple providers seeing patients on roughly the same schedule, there will be peaks where arriving and exiting patients overlap at the check-in desk to create longer than necessary wait times.

Some clinics use check-in to check patients out simply for staffing reasons as the clinic cannot justify the need for more staff or staff another location to manage check-out. Other clinics have not figured out other ways to check patients out with existing staff in more appropriate settings. Many clinics will have a separate check-out station which alleviates the burden of having patients go back to check-in. Other clinics will complete the check-out steps inside the exam room so that patients do not have to make another stop before exiting the clinic.

Do Patients Have to Fill out Paperwork?

Healthcare has paperwork. Some paperwork is for legal reasons, some is to identify each patient, some is to capture patient contact information, and some is to gather more health information on the patient. It is common that forms supplied to patients within the same clinic differ because of different

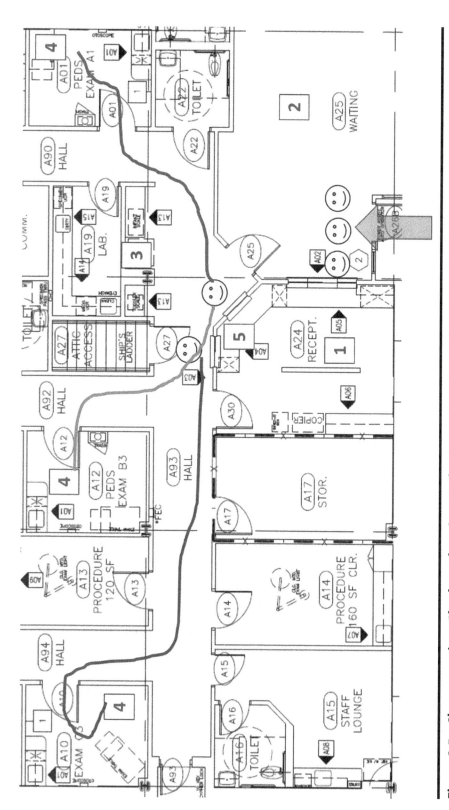

Figure 8.5 Shows a patient Check-out location (5) that is not shared with the patients checking into the clinic (1). The diagram shows the paths three different patients might take after exiting the exam room (4) to Check-out. While the Check-out location is separated from Check-in, it might become congested with patients moving from the waiting room (2) through the door by Check-out and waiting for vitals acquisition in the alcove (3).

providers, different payers, and even different staff working the desk. It is common that forms supplied to patients in different clinics within the same health system vary.

The information collected on the forms is often not necessary and often not collected in the efficient manner the patient prefers. Technology savvy patients likely prefer filling out forms on a mobile device before showing up to an appointment if the form filling is not cumbersome. Other less technology savvy patients may prefer hand filling out forms that arrived through the mail weeks before the appointment. If the forms are not filled out ahead of time, then patients need the time to fill out the forms before the assigned appointment time. If the patient was not allotted time, then he or she may not complete the form or will continue to work on the forms back in the exam room even when staff are working with them. From an efficiency standpoint, forms that are electronically completed are more easily attached or integrated to a patient's universal health record, more easily scored, and more easily incorporated into care planning – as long as the electronic forms are built smartly.

How Long Does Check-in Take?

The check-in process should be a quick process even when there are variables in it. The process can be highly efficient or very clunky depending on how the parts come together and what systems are used. The more effective and efficient the better because patients are not in the clinic for the check-in process. A more effective and efficient process tends to consume less staff time as well.

Excluding any form filling out patients need to complete, a quick check-in process is 1–3 minutes. A process completed by staff in 1.5 minutes as opposed to 3.5 minutes does not sound significant but considering there might be 100 or more patients per day in many clinics, that amounts to 3 hours and 20 minutes less time staff devote to checking in patients per day. Viewed from the patient perspective, a check-in process with form filling that takes only 1.5 minutes in the clinic compared to 13.5 minutes means far less time for the patient to be in the clinic before the appointment time. Those 12 extra minutes across 100 or more patients in a day add up to create the need for more waiting space.

New Patient Check-In Process 1: Steps and Times

Work Step	Description	Low Time Estimate	High Time Estimate
	Patient Arrives		
1	Review ID and DOB	0.5	0.5
2	Updates Insurance and Contact Information	0.5	0.5
3	Pays the CoPay	0.5	0.5
4	Signs Consent to treat and HIPAA forms	0.5	0.5
5	Updates History and Health Screening Forms	5	5
	Patient Waits for Rooming		
	Total Time (Minutes)	7	13.5

New Patient Check-In Process 2: Steps and Times

Work Step	Description	Low Time Estimate	High Time Estimate
	Updates Insurance and Contact Information Updates History and Health Screening Forms Signs Consent to treat and HIPAA forms Patient Arrives		
1	Review ID and DOB	0.5	0.5
2	Pays the CoPay	0.5	0.5
	Patient Waits for Rooming		
	Total Time (Minutes)	1	1.5

Figure 8.6 Shows two different Check-in processes for New Patient Appointments. The process on the left takes more time and resources in the clinic where the process on the right requires some use of technology or mail so the patient can complete work remotely.

How is the Waiting Room?

Waiting rooms come in all shapes, sizes, and levels of comfort, amenities, and aesthetics. By construction code or state law, most clinics will have a waiting room. Though organizations that operate with advance processes and no code obligations could operate without one. Even in patient Self-Rooming clinics, there tends to be some waiting space by building requirement or for the comfort of accompanying family members.

One key way to measure comfort in a waiting space is by counting occupancy in the waiting space and comparing it with the total number of seats or spaces to wait. When a waiting room gets closer and closer to capacity, patients become less comfortable, especially if aesthetics are poor and spacing to the next patient is tight. The more crowded the space feels, the less comfortable it becomes.

Figure 8.7 Shows a picture of a small waiting room equipped with basic seats, couches, and having some ambiance. The waiting room backs up to the Check-in desk that is surrounded by glass to make it more private. The door on the right provides access to the patient care area and medical assistants frequently come in and out of the room collecting the next patient.

Date	10/1/2018			
Day of Week	**Monday**			
Time of Day	**Occupancy**	**Capacity**	**% Utilization**	**Average Time Waiting**
7:30	2	36	5.6%	5
7:40	8	36	22.2%	12
7:50	15	36	41.7%	16
8:00	12	36	33.3%	15
8:10	10	36	27.8%	14
8:20	6	36	16.7%	12
8:30	6	36	16.7%	9
8:40	5	36	13.9%	9
8:50	8	36	22.2%	8
9:00	8	36	22.2%	8
9:10	6	36	16.7%	8
9:20	3	36	8.3%	8
9:30	2	36	5.6%	9
9:40	5	36	13.9%	8
9:50	2	36	5.6%	5
10:00	6	36	16.7%	9
10:10	8	36	22.2%	10

Figure 8.8 Shows a multi-observation data collection sheet of the occupancy of a waiting room compared to the waiting room capacity. Further, the average time waiting in the waiting room was captured, as was the utilization of that space. Simple tables can be extracted from system records or through manual observation.

Another way to evaluate the waiting space experience is by how long patients are in the waiting room. Generally, the longer patients spend in waiting rooms, the greater is the likelihood of patient dissatisfaction. Wait time can be a bit misleading though, because the amount of time patients spend in the waiting room is a function of how early a patient arrives to an appointment (if it is scheduled) and how efficient or on time the provider is managing previous patient visits.

The amount of time a patient spends in the waiting room is not always the same as what some clinics consider patient wait time. For example, Patient A arrives at the clinic at 9 am for a 10 am appointment but the

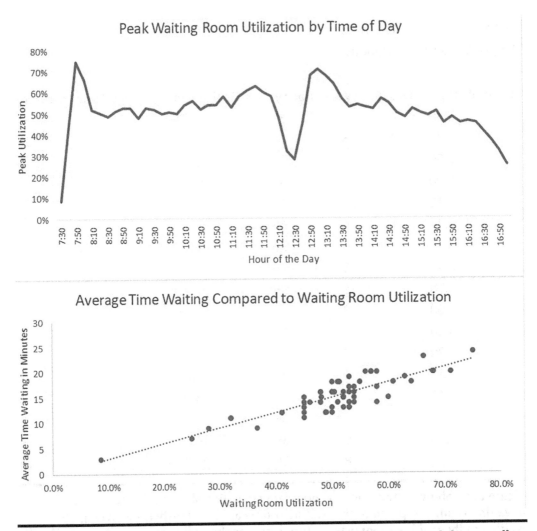

Figure 8.9 Shows the peak waiting room utilization by time of day and the overall utilization peak for space planning purposes. At around 7:50 am the waiting room is filled almost to 80% capacity. Further, a simple scatter plot shows the basic correlation between waiting room utilization and the average amount of time patients wait identifies that each measure tends to increase as the other does. There is nothing surprising here as, when people have to wait longer, more patients will overlap in the queue or in the waiting room.

expected time the patient is to be taken back to the exam room is 9:50 am so the patient is told to arrive by 9:45 am. The actual time Patient A was taken back to the exam room was 9:53 am. In this example the amount of time the patient was waiting in the waiting room was 53 minutes (9:53 am less 9:00 am), the wait time indicator for the patient is 8 minutes (9:53 am less 9:45 am), the clinic is 3 minutes behind schedule (9:53 am less 9:50 am), there is an expected 5 minute wait (9:50 am less 9:45 am), and the patient arrived early by 45 minutes (9:45 am less 9:00 am).

There is nothing wrong with the method above because in scheduled appointment clinics there are certain appointment time expectations shared between clinics and patients. In fact, the methods above can be more useful in understanding patient arrival behavior and process behavior in order to improve the overall experience.

Chapter 9

Questions to Understand how Patients get Roomed

Are Patients Self-Rooming?

If patients physically go to a clinic for care, those patients will get roomed eventually into an exam room or patient care room. While most clinics still have a staff member escort the patient to a patient care room, some organizations have adopted a patient self-rooming model of care. Patient self-rooming is what it sounds like – the patient moves to the patient care room by themselves. In well deployed self-rooming clinics, there is an increase in patient satisfaction because patients avoid a waiting room and there is an increase in staff availability due to less time consumed escorting patients to exam rooms.

The process is not always well received in healthcare but there are plenty of other service industries that use the practice. Hotels generally provide customers with a room key and room number with the expectation that the customer finds the room. Airports allow customers to check-in online, pass through security, and find the gate of departure all by themselves. Further, people are expected to navigate every day on their own whether it is for reasons such as to find a new primary care clinic, to try a new restaurant, or find a friend's new home.

As simple as it sounds, self-rooming can be tricky and not everyone can pull it off. In order to get a patient from the front desk to a patient care room, someone or something must assign the patient a room by knowing what rooms are available for specific providers. Once a patient knows the assigned room, there must be a way for the patient to know where to

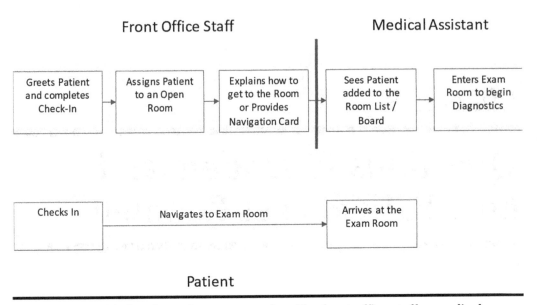

Figure 9.1 **Highlights the main steps completed by front office staff, a medical assistant, and the patient. The self-rooming process is somewhat simple, but front office staff must know which rooms are open and must help patients quickly understand how to navigate to the exam room, and medical assistants must know when a patient arrives at an exam room so as to not delay care. It can be tricky if not thought out.**

go – usually through signage. So that the patient is not stuck waiting for care to begin, staff must know that a patient just roomed themselves to a specific room.

Many organizations choosing self-rooming models have nice on stage/ off stage clinic layouts that make it easy for patients to navigate to an exam room. Organizations that choose self-rooming often rely on the electronic health record system to assign rooms to specific patients and rely on these systems to help communicate between front office and back office staff.

The benefits of patient self-rooming are easily reduced by providers that run chronically behind schedule or clinics that do not have the needed number of exam rooms. Providers that run chronically behind schedule tend to do so because they spend more time with patients than is planned, or they allow for adding on more patients than can be seen on time, or a mix of both.

For Example: Provider Jane Doe is running over 30 minutes behind, as usual. If there are already two patients in patient care rooms (Exam Room 1 and Exam Room 2) awaiting care from provider Jane Doe, another patient is in a patient care room (Exam Room 3) with provider Jane Doe receiving care, and two more patients arrive at the clinic to see Jane Doe, then where do those new patients go? Assuming that there are no more rooms available for provider Jane Doe's patients, those patients have to wait in a waiting room until another room opens before they can self-room. If patients have to wait before self-rooming, then the purpose of self-rooming is somewhat defeated. Assuming that there are other rooms available (Exam Room 4 and Exam Room 5), then the next patients can self-room, but those patients will be waiting in more expensive patient care space rather than a waiting room.

Finally, patient self-rooming is not the be all and end all. Certain markets have patients that prefer a staff escort and certain clinics are designed in a way that means self-rooming would cause more problems than value. Deploying patient self-rooming is a judgment call that can differentiate a clinic by satisfying certain patient segments when it is care and cost appropriate to provide such a rooming option.

Who Escorts the Patient to a Patient Care Room?

Outside of patient self-rooming clinics, a staff member will go into the waiting room, find the patient, and escort that patient eventually to an exam room or patient care room. In most cases, the staff member escorting the patient is the same staff member that will collect vitals and take height/weight measurements. Typically, this staff member is a medical assistant, but they may be a Licensed Practical Nurse, Licensed Vocational Nurse (LPN/LVN), or Registered Nurse (RN), depending on the clinic.

In infrequent cases, the work may get subdivided between a designated patient escort staff member who simply shows patients to a room and a clinical staff member that collects vitals. Usually it is simpler and more efficient to have the escorting staff member also be the person who measures height and weight and acquires vitals, though there are circumstances that escorts make sense. For example, there are clinics that are designed in such a way where the patient has an excessive distance to travel from waiting room to patient care room. In these clinics, the MA must travel a great distance to and from the exam rooms to the waiting room and back. Doing this motion 15–30 times a day for every patient can generate a great deal of time away from supporting the provider and other patients. In order to save that MA motion, patient escorts come in handy. Another case for using escorts is when a clinic is trialing or migrating towards patient self-rooming methods. In these cases, it is often helpful to use escorts in the transition process to help patients find the rooms, or as back-ups to help patients find rooms until the new navigation systems and process are completed.

Where are Height, Weight, and Vitals Acquired?

Some standard clinical information is required most every clinic visit to help the care team evaluate, monitor, and treat each patient. Height and weight are generally the first things measured, followed by temperature, blood pressure, pulse, and often oxygen saturation levels. In clinics there are a variety of locations where this information is collected and different clinical staff members who may collect the measurements. It is common to have height and weight collected in a hallway or alcove on the way from the waiting room to the patient care rooms. It is not as common, but routine enough for clinics to have a vitals collection station or triage area where staff acquire all vitals information prior to getting to the exam room. It is less popular, but growing in popularity, to collect all vitals in the exam room or patient care room.

Clinics equipped to do all measurements and vitals acquisition in the exam room can be more efficient and provide more private personal care.

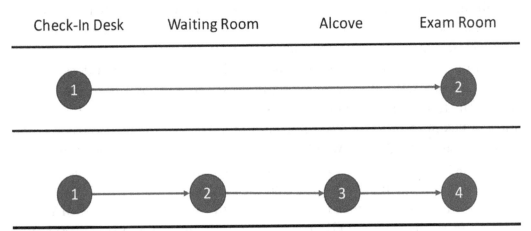

Figure 9.2 Diagrams two different rooming pathways. The pathway on top bypasses the waiting room, height/weight collection stations, and vitals acquisition alcoves because the vitals are acquired in the exam room and patients self-room. The process at the bottom adds a couple more steps for waiting and vitals acquisition in a hallway or alcove.

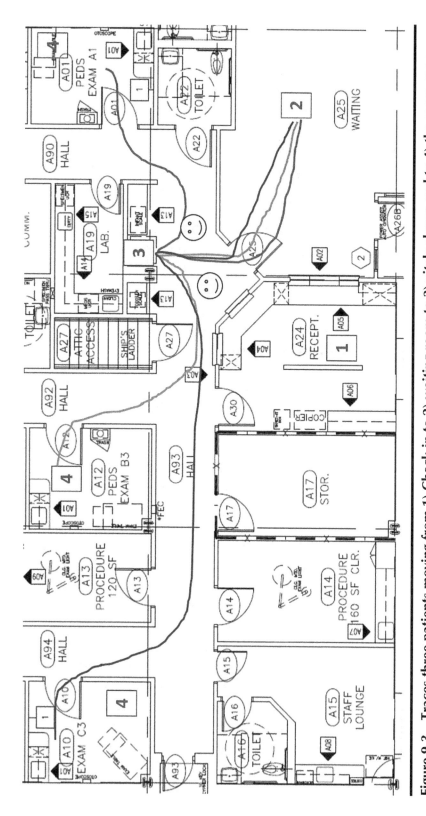

Figure 9.3 Traces three patients moving from 1) Check-in to 2) waiting room to 3) vitals alcove and to 4) the exam room. Vitals collection alcoves create a little extra motion for staff and patients but offer more privacy than a hallway. Even with a well sited alcove location, there can easily be backups in hallways with patients waiting for vitals to be collected. Because alcoves tend to be in logical locations for patient flow, the alcoves can further get congested depending on patients leaving the exam room to Check-out.

Doing all the work in one patient care room means fewer stops for the patient, less motion for staff, less complexity in the process, and usually more privacy. Having a line of patients form behind you at the height/weight scales is less than private. More privacy is often times desired by patients in many geographic areas, though in others it likely makes no difference.

There are simple constraints that prevent some clinics from adopting the practice of doing everything in an exam room. First, many clinics do not have rooms sized, designed, equipped, or laid out in a manner suitable to do everything in one room. Second, not all clinics have invested the capital or have the capital to equip the clinics to do everything in the one room. Third, not all clinics have enough exam rooms to comfortably perform more work in them when the space is needed for the provider to patient interactions. Finally, not all clinics want to trial change.

Who is Discussing a Patient's Reason for the Visit and Current Medications?

Once height and weight are measured, and vitals acquired, a staff member will begin discussing with the patient the reason for the visit – what brought the patient in that day. The conversation is generally not long but enough for the staff member to take notes that prep the provider a little more than what was previously available when the patient scheduled the appointment or spoke to reception. Along with vitals acquisition, the patient's reason for visit discussion may trigger staff to escalate care priorities or transfer the care for a patient immediately. Even in clinics with scheduled appointments, patients can have urgent or emergent issues that need attention as soon as possible that the patient may not be aware of. This is a key point in healthcare that differs from other industries. Even in scheduled care clinics, the planned schedule of the day can be thrown off due to more critical patient care priorities emerging.

After discussing the reason for the visit, a staff member will then typically ask the patient about the different medications and supplements they are taking, how much, and whether prescribed or not. This discussion may identify medication conflicts and helps the care team treat patients safely.

In many clinics, especially Primary Care, a medical assistant will escort the patient, acquire vitals, discuss the reason for the visit and discuss medications. Other organizations may use an LPN/LVN to complete the same work, and some may have a medical assistant escort the patient

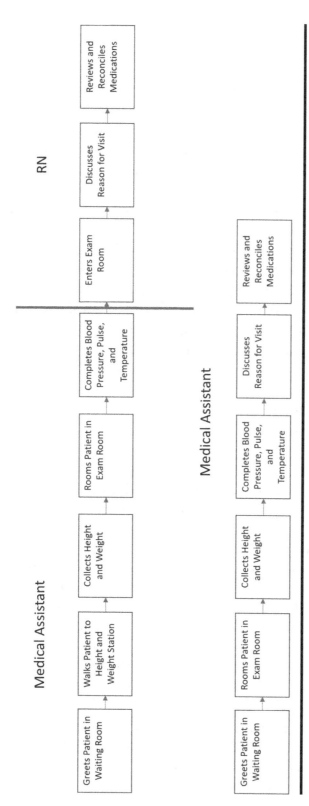

Figure 9.4 Compares two different methods for rooming patients, acquiring vitals, discussing reason for visit, and review current medications. The method on top has a division of responsibility between the medical assistant and RN while the method on the bottom is completed by the medical assistant.

and acquire vitals, but then have an RN discuss the reason for visit and review medications. Each situation, from clinic to clinic, can be different. Ideally, staff are working at the top of what staff are licensed to do. In many cases, a certified medical assistant can manage this whole process. A potential challenge to using MAs to complete the process is that certain geographic regions may not have a large pool of trained certified medical assistants but they have other nurses. Other clinics may have a tougher time attracting well trained medical assistants because of pay or location. Some organizational cultures have a harder time trusting other MAs and other licensed professionals to effectively complete a series of tasks.

In the end, the process of collecting height and weight and acquiring vitals, discussing the reason for visit, and reviewing medications on average takes under ten minutes in most specialties. Multiple staff handoffs involved in this short cycle process can create more errors, delays and miscommunication, and create a blur for the patient who feels like he or she is part of an assembly line being passed around.

Are the Clinical Staff Working at the Top of Licensure?

As mentioned previously, ideally staff should work to the top of what they are licensed to do. That does not mean that staff only work at the top of license, because there is other necessary work to get done that it makes sense for staff to do.

Patients with diabetes tend to get routine foot checks which involve the patient taking off shoes and stockings, and someone completing a physical examination of the feet. One clinic's process allows a medical assistant to complete the review of medications with patients and then leave the exam room. A provider in that clinic then enters the exam room, begins the exam, and at some point has the patient take off shoes and stockings, or has to help the patient do so. At another clinic, the medical assistant stays in the exam room after the review of medications and helps the patient to remove shoes and stockings to prep that patient for the physical exam. At a third clinic, a medical assistant stays in the exam room after the review of medications, helps the patient to remove shoes and stockings, performs the foot check, and documents the findings for the provider that will soon enter providing oversight.

The third clinic in the example above allows the provider to do more work at the top of a provider's license while it allows a medical assistant to perform higher level tasks even if that means helping to remove patient shoes and stockings first. The third clinic in the example above freed providers' time up to do more important care tasks which might be seeing more patients, spending more valuable time with each patient, or completing the additional four hours of afterhours patient documentation earlier each day.

Ideally, staff should work to the top of what they are licensed to do. In reality, it will depend. For billing purposes or clinical competency reasons, often the provider must be the one to complete certain patient care work. While there is little a clinic can do with licensure and billing restrictions, competency limitations are something that can be managed.

Are Patients Stopping for Collections First or at the End?

For specific appointment types or because of the reasons for a patient to visit, some care tasks are standardized in clinics. Clinics that define the standard care tasks tend to call the standard tasks "protocols". Protocols simply allow staff to execute more work without waiting for the provider to direct each step. Protocols can allow a clinic to be more proactive and help staff to work towards the top of licensure. Of course, if not designed well, protocols can create excessive work and unnecessary tests too. For example, patients coming to a clinic for a new job or work physical that includes a drug screening should not have to wait until after the provider exam to complete the urinalysis. In many cases, the urinalysis collection can be completed right after check-in by stopping at the bathroom on the way to the exam room from the waiting room.

How Do the Clinical Staff Alert the Provider that the Patient is Ready?

The question above sounds simple but in reality, clinical support staff and the providers work together without physically seeing each other for periods of time.

For example: Provider Jane Doe is finishing the exam for Patient A in Room 5, while medical assistant James Smith is discussing the reason for visit with Patient C in Room 6, then the provider Jane Doe leaves Room 5 to start the exam for Patient B, already roomed and prepped in Room 4.

The example above may happen continuously in a given day when a provider and his or her staff are not face to face. Learning how the care team communicates between members without being face to face is a great indicator of how effective and efficient the team is. Plenty of clinics still use color-coded exam room door flags and fewer may even couple the flag system with provider name placards to dynamically notify providers the next room to enter when rooms are not pre-assigned for the day. Many clinics have folder trays hanging from exam room doors which hold folders or charts that notify the provider of the next room. Many clinics use notes and electronic flag systems within the electronic health record. Others may use large TVs displaying the room assignments.

The methods of communication between staff and providers will vary from clinic to clinic, so it is important to identify the methods and uncover any miscommunications, gaps, or inefficiencies in the methods. Flag systems on doors are simple and effective but often times not consistently used. Flag or notification systems in the EMR are also simple but require staff and providers to be in front of a computer screen to use them. If providers or staff do not have portable technology to view the EMR, then the team will frequently have to walk back to a computer station.

Chapter 10

Questions to Understand the Provider Exam and Provider Workflow

How Much Time do Providers Spend in the Exam Room with Patients?

Once the provider arrives at the exam room, a patient can expect various engagement styles, different amounts of time in the exam room, and a variety of comfort. The provider will ultimately want to understand the reason for the visit, understand medical history, current conditions, current medications, and then complete a physical exam to inspect specific body systems. The first part is a question and answer session followed by a physical exam, though the two may get somewhat blended together.

Once the physical exam is completed, the provider may be able to readily explain what they found and explain what they recommend for treatment if treatment is warranted. Depending on information available and complexities, the provider may leave the exam room and then return before explaining what they assessed or what the recommended treatment is. If prescriptions or other tests need to be ordered, some providers might complete those orders while in the room with the patient while others may finish the orders after the patient has left before seeing the next patient. There are varying practice patterns for each provider and situation.

More times than not, patients go to a clinic for treatment, advice, and to see a provider. Therefore, the time spent with the provider is the "main event" for the patient. The amount of time spent with the patient is just as important

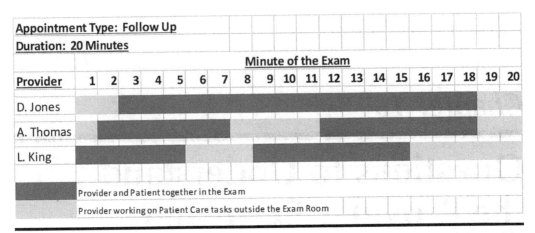

Figure 10.1   Illustrates how different providers spend different amounts of time with patients in the exam room and the number of times a provider leaves and comes back. Each patient may require a different pattern of work due to the nature of the reason for visit, but overall when looking at enough like type patients, patterns tend to emerge.

as the quality of that time spent with the patient. When a patient feels rushed or if time is limited with the provider, then patients tend to become dissatisfied. When the amount of time a patient spends with a provider is a small percentage of the total time it took them to travel to the clinic, to wait in the waiting room, and to wait alone in the exam room, then patients tend to become dissatisfied. Likewise, the amount of time a provider spends with each patient in the exam room should be a large chunk of the total work time he or she spends on each patient, if the processes are efficient.

How Much Documentation do Providers Complete in the Exam Room with the Patient?

For each visit, the provider is not just engaging with a vulnerable patient, quickly determining what is wrong, and readily determining treatment, each provider must thoroughly document everything in a Visit Note. Documentation is important for recording care history and informing care across the continuum, and it is also a key component to reimbursement.

Documentation styles generally differ from provider to provider as does the speed and efficiency of documentation. Providers may document with a pen, use a keyboard, leverage voice recognition software, or have someone

Collected Work Times: In Minutes Provider Studied: A. Thomas				
Patient	Patient Care Time in Exam Room	Patient Care Time Outside Exam Room	Other Patient Care Documentation Time	Total
Patient 1	13	7	15	35
Patient 2	14	5	20	39
		Continues		
Patient 50	16	5	12	33
Average	14.3	5.7	15.7	35.7
% of Total	40.2%	15.9%	43.9%	

Figure 10.2   Shows the amount of work time a specific provider spent on each patient over the course of seeing 50 patients during a few days in clinic. About 40% of the work time is in the exam room with the patient, almost 16% of the work time is completed outside the exam room during clinic, and almost another 40% of the work time is completing documentation or reviews after clinic hours. In the above case, A. Thomas has a large amount of documentation to complete after clinic hours.

else entirely do the bulk of the documentation. Documentation itself may follow a similar general format like Subjective-Objective-Assessment-Plan (SOAP), but specifics within the note may be different per provider or different by patient or different by reason for the patient visit. Some providers are more thorough in documentation than others and some may just use more words than others.

Many providers do not wait until patients leave to begin documentation and, in many cases, it is a good practice to engage the patient in explaining or showing what is being documented. In these cases, providers will document in the exam room with the patient, which is no simple task, holding a conversation while clicking or typing.

Learning how much time a provider spends documenting while in the exam room and how that time compares to the total time spent documenting per patient will help identify how efficient the documentation process is. Further, it is helpful to learn approximately how much work time providers spend documenting or working in the EMR compared to engaging with the patient in the exam room. Ideally, a larger chunk of time is spent engaging with patients rather than working in the EMR, but some systems are better than others.

How Much Time are Providers Spending in Motion Between Exam Rooms?

Providers typically do not spend a great deal of time with each patient. On average, Surgical Specialists may spend 5–10 minutes with each patient, Primary Care providers may spend 15–30 minutes, and some Medical Specialists may spend 45–75 minutes with each patient. It really depends. If a Primary Care provider spends 30 seconds walking between exam rooms to see each patient, another 30 seconds moving to and from a printer outside the exam room for each patient, and another 30 seconds walking to and from a computer outside the exam room for each patient, then that provider has already spent what is equal to 5%–10% of the amount of time that the provider spends with each patient. That time is necessary, but not as valuable as the time spent with patients. Time in motion all adds up.

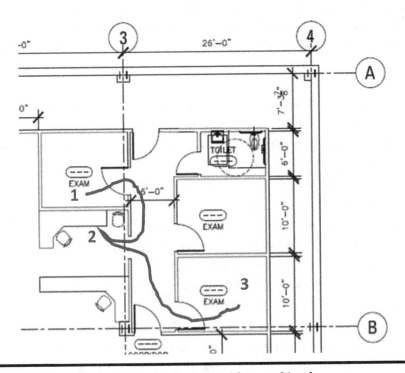

Figure 10.3 Shows the work paths for a provider working between exam rooms (1 and 3) and a charting station (2). In this clinic the provider is assigned three rooms and works out of the exam rooms and nearby charting station with her medical assistant. The proximity from the charting station to the assigned exam rooms is minimal and reduces some motion.

There are many reasons for the excess movement. Often clinics are poorly designed and, depending on room assignments, providers just have a great deal of walking to do. Some clinics may have good room assignments, but the printer and provider charting station is not close or right outside the exam rooms. Often clinics do not equip exam rooms with enough equipment or resources to keep the providers from having to leave the exam room. The reasons for the excess motion are numerous, important to know, and should be opportunities to improve. Often times it is the countless little things that add up to be the biggest problem.

How Much Time are Providers Spending on Patient Care Tasks Outside the Exam Room Between Patients?

Knowing just the amount of patient care time a provider spends with each patient in the exam room is not enough because many patient care tasks can occur outside the exam room. Providers routinely leave an exam room, complete patient care tasks, and come back to the exam room during one patient visit. Providers routinely discharge a patient from the exam room and complete patient care work for that patient before moving on to the next patient.

Depending on how the provider works, those outside of the exam room Tasks can be any number of things. A provider may order a patient some prescriptions as soon as a patient is discharged, or a provider might step out following the physical exam to call another clinic or provider to discuss a patient's history. A provider may need to step out of the room to privately review information or even research treatment options. These tasks are usually completed at a provider charting station nearby the exam rooms or even in the provider's office should he or she have one.

Learning how much patient care work occurs outside the exam room between patients, will help identify the work cycle time per provider. The amount of time a provider spends in the exam room with a patient plus the amount of time the provider spends on patient care tasks for that patient outside the exam room before moving to the next patient, is one way to measure a provider's Cycle Time – it is the provider's pace per patient.

To assess the full work time per each patient that visits, add in the amount of time a provider works (usually documentation) outside patient care hours in the clinic. Usually this is the time after the last patient leaves, lunch time, or before the first patient arrives in the morning.

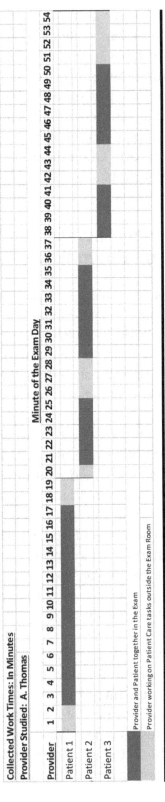

Figure 10.4   Time maps of the amount of time a provider spends working with patients in the exam room and outside the exam room beforehand. A. Thomas spent 15 minutes with Patient 1 in the exam room and 19 minutes on Patient 1 before moving on to Patient 2. A. Thomas spent 12 minutes with Patient 2 in the exam room and 18 minutes on Patient 2 before moving on to Patient 3. A. Thomas spent 10 minutes with Patient 3 in the exam room and 17 minutes on Patient 3 before moving on to the next patient.

Appointment Type: Follow Up				
Duration: 20 Minutes				
Provider: J. Doe				
Appointment Type	**Scheduled Duration**	**A. Exam Room Cycle Time**	**B. During Clinic Cycle Time**	**C. Total Cycle Time**
Acute	15	15	19	27
Follow Up / Routine	30	18	21	29
New Patient	60	26	40	55

Figure 10.5   Shows the amount of time scheduled for a provider's appointments compared to the actual time spent, based on three common work times. A. Exam room cycle time is the amount of time the provider spends with patients in the exam room. B. During clinic cycle time is the amount of time a provider spends on patient care inside and outside the exam room as illustrated in Figure 10.4. C. Total work time further adds in the after hours documentation and work completed for each patient. In the example, Provider J. Doe spends more time on acute appointments than scheduled while spending less time than scheduled on follow-up appointments and New Patient Appointments.

Is the Exam Room Set Up for Good Interaction Between Patient and Caregiver?

Electronic documentation of patient care records has created a need to have computers in the exam room. As the burden of documentation can be heavy, many providers document as they talk or examine the patient just as they might take handwritten notes in years past. The challenge with computers is that they tend to be larger, tend to need power, and tend to need an internet connection.

Some organizations do not give the computer placement, the exam table, and where the patient sits when not on the exam table much thought. What happens in these organizations is that a provider either has to turn his or her back to the patient to document or has to contort at some awkward

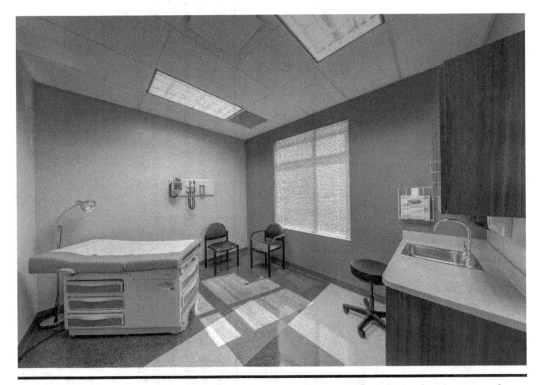

Figure 10.6   Shows a basic exam room in a Family Medicine clinic that is set up for good patient to provider interaction without much else. When the provider enters the exam room, the patient is likely in the chair under the vitals equipment mounted on the wall, where the medical assistant collected vitals. The provider uses the mobile stool, laptop on lap or laptop on potable cart to engage with the patient eye to eye. When it is time to conduct the physical exam, the provider will help the patient onto the exam table.

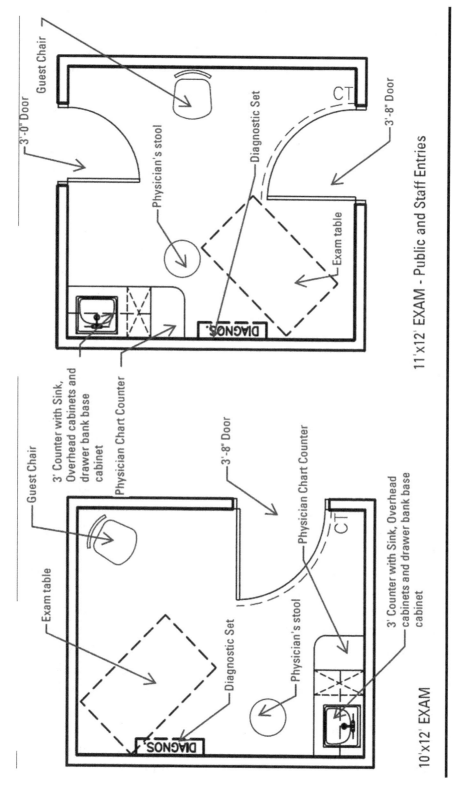

11'x12' EXAM - Public and Staff Entries

10'x12' EXAM

Figure 10.7 Shows two simple layouts for exam rooms that allow patients to interact with providers using portable documentation methods like laptops and portable carts. The room on the left is more traditional while the room on the right allows for dual access to the room for on stage/off stage processes. Also to note, each exam room has a door swing that shields the exam table and provides privacy to patients should the door open during a physical exam.

angle to engage eye to eye when documenting. Neither is ideal for the patient or provider.

Many organizations have adopted handy sized laptops for providers to tote from room to room. Some organizations offer providers mini mobile workstations to roll right up in front or beside a patient. Other organizations have gone the distance to set up mini conference stations in each exam room so that a provider maintains good eye contact with the patient but also allows the patient so see what the provider is documenting by projecting on a wall mounted TV screen. The provider may share notes, lab results, or even create a remote consult to another provider on the spot in these situations.

As mentioned earlier, patients go to a clinic for treatment, advice, and to engage with a provider. When a provider spends more time looking at a computer screen than at the patient or when a provider has his or her back routinely to a patient, then generally a patient feels less engaged and dissatisfied.

Do Providers Use Scribes, Dictation, or Voice Recognition?

So that providers do not document during the patient exam, many organizations and providers use scribes. Scribes document what the patient and provider are discussing in the exam room, retrieve test results in the EMR, and realistically do most EMR functions for the provider so the provider spends minimal time with those data entry tasks. Usually scribes do not enter orders for providers, but they potentially could under certain circumstances or could at least start them. Scribes can be a great efficiency boost for many providers, a great satisfier for providers who hate documentation, but they come at a cost of having extra staff. For many providers and specialties, the boost in efficiency and provider satisfaction outweighs the cost, but not always.

Dictation processes and voice recognition software are frequently used to reduce the amount of time providers spend documenting. A dictation process allows a provider to speak everything he or she wants included in the visit note and someone or something else will transcribe that visit note in electronic format. Voice recognition software completes the transcription process in mostly real time while the provider dictates, while traditional dictation processes have a delay between dictation and transcription.

Voice recognition software increases many providers' efficiency in documenting while frustrating other providers. There is a learning curve and usually some training for providers to fully accept these options, if the provider will accept the options at all. The use of dictation processes and voice recognition come at extra costs which many times makes sense while at others it does not.

Learning what solutions and systems are used to aid providers in documentation can explain a great deal about the extent to which an organization will go to satisfy providers and make them more productive. Learning how well the solutions and systems were deployed can further explain how well an organization adopted the systems or how effectively the systems were rolled out.

How Does a Provider let Clinical Staff Know that they Need Something During an Exam?

Whether planned or not, providers need different supplies and equipment for different patients. Proactive provider care teams tend to work ahead and prepare rooms adequately. Proactive provider care teams tend to communicate efficiently. Other care teams may regularly forget to stock rooms adequately or forget key equipment thereby causing the provider to stop in the middle of care to retrieve or request the missing need. Many times these disruptions are minimal while others are more time consuming. Some organizations' disruptions are frequent while in others they rarely happen.

If or when there is a disruption to a provider's workflow, a provider may have to physically leave the exam and go find help. Help may be in the form of an MA nearby or a supply closet down the hall. In other cases, organizations might use the "Red Flag" on the door flag system so that a provider alerts staff that there is an urgent need. Some organizations deploy technology solutions like a nurse call alert or push button alarms that notify staff of a need.

Learning how often providers must stop to retrieve or request help can explain how much provider efficiency is lost. Organizations with providers that must stop frequently and for longer periods of time are not efficient or proactive. There are plenty of simple processes to minimize these disruptions. As mentioned before, sometimes it is the countless little things that add up to be an organization's biggest problem.

How Does the Provider Give the Patient Closure?

The question here is another simple and subtle one, but important. Patients are not as familiar with clinic processes as a provider is nor do many patients know their provider's behavior well. Patients don't always know when the appointment is over because it is not a process the patient is in control of. Patients might still sit in the exam room after the provider and staff have left the room because the appointment was over for them. The patient might remain unsure of whether the provider or staff told them to leave, where to go next, or what after that. After a while, patients pop a head out of the exam room and ask if they can go. This usually happens because of a lack of closure.

Providers hold a powerful role for a patient, so when a patient does not get the information needed and the cue to leave, then patients are likely to simply stay put. Patients need information on the next steps in treatment or care but also need to know very simply what to do next right now in the clinic. Whether that is waiting for MA Jones to come back in to release them or to walk back up to the front desk. The cue from a provider is the simple notification that the exam is over and he or she will not be back in the room again. People say goodbye in different ways, but they still say goodbye.

Chapter 11

Questions to Understand Patient Discharge and Patient Treatment

Who Schedules Treatments, Follow-up Appointments, or Further Care for the Patient?

Many patients will not need further planned care after seeing a provider until their next Annual Wellness review. Other patients may need extensive follow-on appointments and care services. While clinic staff are generally busy, it is a good practice to help patients schedule as much of the follow-up care as makes sense – usually the near term services. In many clinics that offer this service, a front office staff member schedules follow-on care while in other organizations a back office staff member schedules follow-on appointments right before discharging the patient from the exam room. Other clinics will point the patient to a central scheduling hotline or hand over a list of providers the clinic recommends as the places to receive care.

When forward scheduling is not done well enough for patients, those patients tend to call back to the clinic, message the clinic through the EMR, or even incorrectly try to schedule follow-up care. Scheduling rework is costly because it is time consuming and it is also disruptive during a busy day to stop work and answer calls or reply to messages. Sometimes forward scheduling is done excessively by organizations. These organizations may require that all follow-on care for a patient is scheduled before leaving the clinic, even when the next appointment is six months or a year out. In many cases, the patient does not remember the appointment, did not realize an appointment was even scheduled, or remembers but must call back to reschedule. Learning who and how well forward scheduling is done helps identify where rework and inefficiencies exist.

Who Completes and Where are the After Visit Summary and Discharge Completed?

The After Visit Summary (AVS) comes in many formats, but serves as a reminder to the patient why he or she had an appointment, what the outcome of the appointment was, what further medications, treatments, or appointments the patient needs to make, what the follow-up plan is, and more. The AVS has learning information for each patient and when reviewed in the clinic it serves as an opportunity to discuss care questions with the patient. When an AVS is created and delivered well, the patient is well informed and can navigate next steps alone. When an AVS is not created or delivered well, patients tend to call back to the clinic asking questions, which generates rework for staff, or worse outcomes occur when patients do not follow the instructions.

There are many ways the process is completed. First, a provider may prefer to print and review the AVS with each patient before discharging the patient. In this process, the provider fields any questions and reviews the main points. The AVS in this review process will not have follow-on appointment dates listed, because no one has scheduled those yet, but there can be a list of follow-on appointments to make.

Second, a provider may give a patient closure in the exam and then turn over discharge to a medical assistant. The MA might schedule appropriate follow-up care, review the AVS with the patient, and then discharge the patient from the exam room and clinic. In this process, the AVS will have some follow-on appointment dates listed and a list of other follow-on appointments to be scheduled. This process is similar to good Acute Care discharging processes at the bedside in a hospital, though some clinics dislike the idea of tying up MA time in follow-on scheduling.

Third, another provider may give a patient closure in the exam room and then send the patient to the check-out desk. At the check-out desk, a front office staff member may schedule follow-on appointments for the patient, print the AVS, and discharge the patient. In this process there is usually less

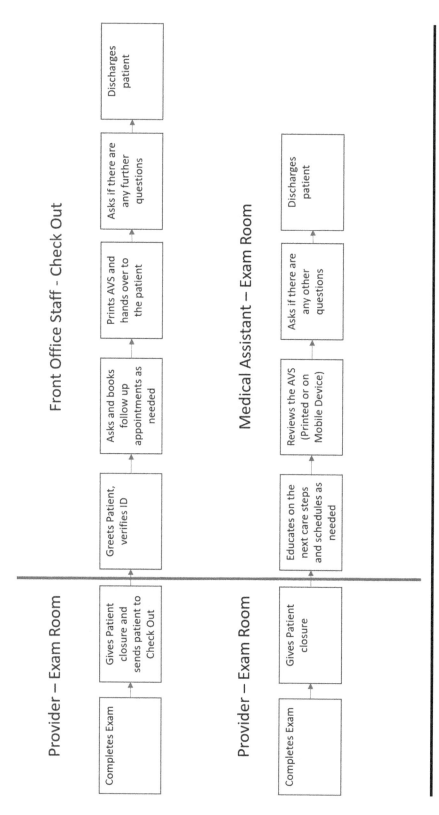

Front Office Staff - Check Out

Provider – Exam Room

Completes Exam → Gives Patient closure and sends patient to Check Out → Greets Patient, verifies ID → Asks and books follow up appointments as needed → Prints AVS and hands over to the patient → Asks if there are any further questions → Discharges patient

Medical Assistant – Exam Room

Provider – Exam Room

Completes Exam → Gives Patient closure → Educates on the next care steps and schedules as needed → Reviews the AVS (Printed or on Mobile Device) → Asks if there are any other questions → Discharges patient

Figure 11.1   Shows two different processes for providing closure, reviewing the AVS, scheduling, and discharging a patient. The process on the top does not tie up the medical assistant or the exam room to complete the discharge tasks. The process on the bottom keeps the patient in the private exam room to provide better education, provide a better patient experience, and to reduce the number of messages or phone calls patients make after a visit.

privacy to discuss any questions about the AVS. Further, the front office staff are not usually clinical staff so many questions or concerns cannot be properly fielded by front office staff. In this option, having the front office staff schedule follow-on appointments frees up clinical staff and exam room time.

Finally, there are any number of variations and modifications to the three listed above. Some options promote resource efficiency over quality. Some promote thoroughness over timeliness.

Chapter 12

Questions to Understand Patient Care Happening Between Visits

How are Refills Managed?

Just because patients are not present in a clinic does not mean that care for them stops. Patients prescribed medications for acute or chronic conditions frequently need refills before the next follow-up appointment. Providers and clinics that manage care for a large population of patients with chronic conditions can be overwhelmed with refill requests.

Many clinics have staff that support one provider and those staff manage the refill requests for that provider's patients. Many clinics designate staff to manage all the refills for all providers in the clinic. In smaller clinics with fewer refill requests, it does not make much sense to have separate staff, but in larger clinics with a high volume of refill requests, it may work best to have devoted staff to manage them. In some organizations the dedicated refill request staff report through the RN Care Coordinator or care manager team because the focus of that team is typically all care outside the clinic walls, to include refills, follow-up compliance, rechecks, and other care events.

Who Manages Email or Phone Traffic?

Phone lines and email message baskets in a clinic can become very busy with incoming contact from patients, other providers, businesses, salespeople, administrators, and many more people. Some calls or messages should go to a clinical staff member while others should be fielded by front office staff, and others must be handled by a provider. Unfortunately, often due to processes or constraints on the number of phone lines in a clinic, the person that needs to handle the call or message may be the second, third, or fourth person brought into the call or message. An unnecessary amount of staff time is consumed in this activity. Further, phone calls and messages are also a disruptive form of communication because they can break a person's concentration on the task at hand.

Organizations deploy different techniques to minimize these impacts. Some organizations maintain one published phone number that is managed by a front office staff member who triages all calls before handling the call or handing off the call to clinical staff. Some organizations maintain two published phone lines with the first being a front office public line and the second being a back office private line dedicated to provider to provider or clinical staff use only between clinics. Secure email is generally managed with front office staff and back office staff acting as triage agents or screeners before messages are released to providers or other staff.

Learning how organizations manage all the offline patient care traffic and how well it is managed will help identify how productive a clinic is. It may also explain how stressed a particular clinic is too.

How Much Outreach is Completed?

In many clinics there is a push to keep patients healthy or as well as possible. Because care does not stop once a patient leaves a clinic, clinics tend to keep a pulse on patients outside the clinic. Besides Annual Wellness visits or routine chronic condition checks, many clinics frequently reach out to engage patients remotely. The outreach may include a reminder to get appropriate preventive tests or checks completed, a reminder to book an Annual Wellness visit, a request to complete a current health questionnaire, or a push to update annual health goals or to educate on specific health issues.

The outreach may be conducted via a follow-up phone call for a patient that had been in the Emergency Room. The outreach may be done as an in person visit by an RN Care Coordinator to a patient recently admitted to a Hospital. The outreach may be an email message by staff trying to find out why a patient did not complete the prescribed follow-up care services or staff trying to help a patient schedule follow-up care.

Useful outreach can provide value to both patients and the clinic. At the same time, someone from the team must complete the outreach and must oversee the outreach. Outreach might be completed by each medical assistant assigned to a specific provider. Outreach might be completed by a designated staff member reaching out to every providers' patients. Outreach might be completed by an RN Care Coordinator keeping a pulse on all patients. In reality, outreach might be completed by all the options. Learning what outreach is done, how effective the outreach is, and how efficient the outreach is can identify some important gaps.

KEY CAPACITY CONCEPTS AND VARIABLES TO ASSESS

Chapter 13

Questions to Understand the Care Team

Who is Part of the Care Team?

The care team is a mix of staff that serve the patient from before each visit, during each visit, and between visits. Care team members include physicians, mid-level providers, ancillary providers, RNs, LPN/LVNs, MAs, front office staff and other ancillary staff. The mix of staff and each staff member's role varies often from clinic to clinic and specialty to specialty. Some care teams are comprised simply of a provider and a medical assistant while another has a physician, a physician's assistant extender, an RN, a medical assistant, and front office staff. Ideally, each member of the care team can work at the top of what he or she is licensed to do and is appropriately utilized for value added activities.

The mix and responsibilities of each care team member often align with how an organization is paid and the specialty service provided. For example, an FFS clinic may have physicians who are each assigned one MA and supported by minimal front office staff. The clinic is paid off office visits, so the care team is centered around having patients physically visit the office. Clinics under a capitated population health program may have physicians that work with one MA supported by front office staff to manage patient visits, and work with RN Care Coordinators for patients between care visits. The capitated clinic is paid by the number of patient members managed, and incentivized further when Emergency Rooms or Hospitals are not used by patients. Having additional staff resources to proactively manage care outside the clinic visit pays off.

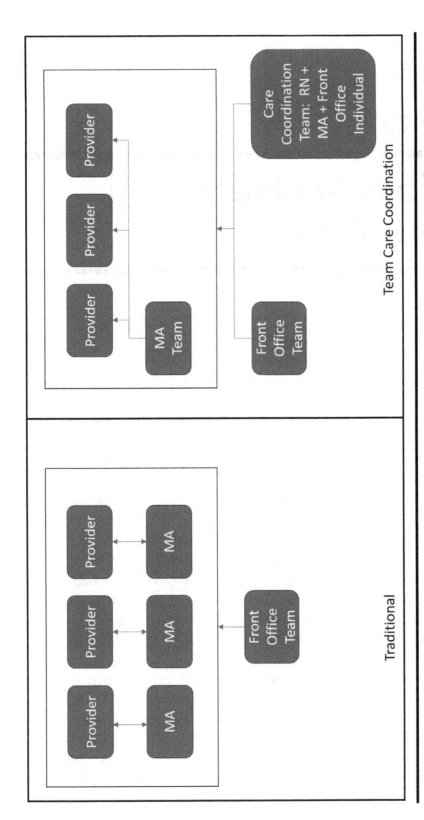

Figure 13.1 Shows two different care team models though there are countless others. In the "Traditional" model on the left, an MA is designated to support one provider while a team of front office staff supports all providers. In the "Traditional" model, the designated MA manages all of the pre-visit, during visit, and between visit activities for patients assigned to his or her provider. In the "Team Care Coordination" model on the right, a pool of MAs supports all providers in the clinic for all of the during visit tasks for the patient visit. A smaller front office team still supports all providers with a focus on during visit tasks and a care coordination team does a bulk of the work on pre-visit and between visit tasks for all providers.

Learning the composition of the care team and the responsibilities of the care team will inform how the clinic cares for its patients. Because staffing is the largest cost for clinics, the care team model will identify the overarching costs of a clinic too.

How do the Providers Act as Part of the Larger Care Team?

Many patients prefer having one designated provider or, in Primary Care, a Primary Care Provider (PCP). Some patients don't really worry about having one designated PCP or provider as long as they get care when they need it. Some providers only want to see patients assigned to them and other providers are comfortable seeing any patient that visits or managing care for a pool of patients with other providers. Because of these different preferences and differences in how providers are paid, there are different participation styles for providers in each clinic.

Providers that only want to see assigned patients are best matched to patients that want access to one designated provider or PCP. This relationship works as long as there are enough patients who prefer the personality of a specific provider or PCP and the patients have enough access to that provider. Consider that providers are regular people with a life, vacations, family, emergencies, and daily routines that can keep them from working 24/7/365. When a designated provider is not available for care, a clinic might try to book patients' future appointments or may allow for direct messaging between patient and provider at certain hours. The reality is, the provider will not be available all the time, so when issues arise and the designated provider cannot respond quickly enough, then patients might choose alternatives.

Providers that are comfortable seeing any patient that visits or managing care for a pool of patients with other providers are good to match with patients that don't really care to have one designated provider or PCP as long as they get care when they need it. These providers are also good to pair with other designated providers so as to provide coverage when designated providers are not available for coverage to patients. These providers may work in a team of other providers or might act as a backup or as an extender for a designated provider.

In the end, it is a balance between having flexibility to offer availability and dedicated personalized care. Learning how providers work in the greater team will identify whether the flexibility and dedication satisfy patient demands or preferences.

Chapter 14

Questions to Understand Patient Scheduling and Provider Schedules

How Much Time do Providers Book for Each Visit or Allocate per Patient?

Providers work at different paces and some reasons why patients visit a clinic require more time than others. There is also variability in care and patient engagement. Many clinics will plan for a certain amount of time for all patient appointments or visits. For example, a walk-in clinic may plan that all visits will take on average 15 minutes or an appointment based Family Medicine clinic may plan 20 minutes for any patient visit. Other appointment based clinics will vary the planned visit times by provider and type of appointment. *For example, provider Jane Doe in Clinic A blocks 60 minutes for New Patient appointments, 15 minutes for Same Day acute appointments, and 30 minutes for follow-up appointments while her clinic colleague provider Bob Jones blocks 40 minutes, 10 minutes, and 20 minutes respectively.*

The amount of time clinics plan or block out for certain appointments should on average match the amount of time the provider spends for each visit. When planned time does not match actual, then problems can arise that we will discuss later.

Clinics that block different times for different appointments and providers can make scheduling complex for front office staff who speak to patients and schedule. The complexity breeds front office staff who must become very specialized in specific clinic and providers' practices. Clinics with one appointment duration are rather simple to schedule but run the risk of creating a clinic day that runs behind because too many appointments were under-scheduled.

How do Providers Schedule the Care Day?

Clinics and providers use various strategies to schedule or plan the care day. Clinics that do not use one uniform appointment time duration often create complex daily schedule templates for front office staff to follow. The templates tell front office schedulers how many of which type of appointments to fit at what times of the day. The templates might also restrict some appointments at certain times of the day or restrict certain appointments from following certain other appointment types. Precision scheduling is done by provider preference. Often providers prefer a certain order to the day so as to not fall behind or feel overwhelmed. There are many clinics that pull off precision scheduling well, especially when the template still allows for considerable patient access to care. For other clinics, the complexity involved in achieving the precision schedule is not always worth it because it can restrict patient access or create chronic daily backlogs because the time scheduled per visit doesn't come close to what actually occurs.

Some clinics that use one uniform appointment time actually restrict or impose scheduling rules to follow. Because some reasons for patients to visit actually do require different amounts of time for a provider, these rules accommodate the provider's preference and ability to stay on time. While these schedules are not necessarily restricted as much as the method mentioned above, this method is restricted but allows a front office scheduler to schedule patients without having to seek as much advice or spend time specializing. For example, a scheduler may be required to book longer and more complex visits, like New Patient Appointments, at the start of each hour followed by quicker, less complex visits, such as Same Day acute. The idea is that the scheduled day stays on time, on average, hourly throughout the day. Many clinics successfully pull off this simpler schedule and tend not to restrict patient access to care much. Other clinics cannot successfully deploy the simpler method because providers are not working at the planned pace and are not structured to do so.

Day of the Week: Tuesday
Provider: J. Doe

Time Slot	Specific Appointments	Restriction Notes
8:00	Acute	1) Hold 2 slots in the morning for Same Day Acute Appointments 2) No more than 2 New Patient Appointments per day at blocks indicated 3) Acute appointments require 1 slot or 10 minutes 4) New Patient Appointments require 4 slots or 40 minutes 5) all other appointments are 2 slots or 20 minutes
8:10	Acute	
8:20		
8:30		
8:40		
8:50		
9:00	New	
9:10		
9:20		
9:30		
9:40		
9:50		
10:00		
10:10		

Day of the Week: Tuesday
Provider: A. Thomas

Time Slot	Specific Appointments	Restriction Notes
8:00	Long	1) All appointments block 20 minutes 2) New Patient appointments, physicals, wellness checks go at the top of the hour 2) Acute Same Day appointments, values checks, and simple follow ups go next 3) all other routine visits go at the end of the hour
8:20	Short	
8:40	Normal	
9:00	Long	
9:20	Short	
9:40	Normal	
10:00	Long	

Figure 14.1 Shows two different providers' templated schedules. Provider J. Doe on the left has 10 minute time slots and uses 10 minute acute blocks, 20 minute routine blocks, and 40 minute New Patient blocks to fill the schedule. J. Doe holds two slots at 8am for acute Same Day appointments and one block at 9am for New Patients. Provider A. Thomas on the right uses 20 minute blocks for everything but requires a specific sequence to the appointments.

A less restrictive form of scheduling is open scheduling. Open scheduling generally uses one uniform time block, though it is not mandatory. Schedulers can insert any patient appointment on any part of the schedule, with an emphasis on getting the patient seen as soon as possible at the patient's preference. There is less emphasis on scheduling future follow-on care and often guidance against it, so the schedule stays truly open because some have learned that scheduling too far out just creates rework. Open scheduling is very simple in concept and process but often hard to implement culturally. Many clinics prefer to book out as much provider time in advance as possible and control when certain appointments are completed. Many clinics running under capitated reimbursement plans deploy open scheduling more successfully because an FFS clinic has to get past the leap of faith that a relatively open schedule, going into the clinic day, will fill up with today's needs.

Is there a Difference Between Time Scheduled or Allocated per Patient and What is Used?

In scheduled clinics, the patient schedule establishes the planned throughput for each day, week, and over the year. Comparing what was planned in the schedule to what happens can identify opportunities to increase throughput or adjust to better stay on time. Comparing planned versus actual will identify difference.

In order to identify difference, compare the amount of time a provider spends on each patient per appointment to the amount of time scheduled. As explained in Chapter 8, the work and cycle times useful in the comparison are a) the total time a provider spends in the exam room with the patient b) the total time a provider spends on patient care tasks for a patient during the clinic day and c) total time to include afterhours documentation. Ideally, "b" is the best option to use in the comparison.

When comparing the work cycle times to the scheduled amount of time per patient visit, there usually is quite a bit of variation if the data comes from clinics that choose to have one uniform time duration. While there is typically difference in each comparison, when you sum up that difference over a days' worth of visits, the overall daily difference should be minimal. When comparing data from a clinic that chooses more precision scheduling methods, there should not be as much variation and difference for each comparison. Likewise, when you sum up that difference over a days' worth of visits, the overall difference should be minimal.

Day of the Week: Monday			
Provider: J. Doe			
Unit of Measure: Minutes			
Patient	Scheduled Time Duration	b) Provider Cycle for Patient Care Time in Clinic	Bias
Patient 1	20	26	-6
Patient 2	20	14	6
Patient 3	20	19	1
	Continues		
Patient 22	20	28	-8
Patient 23	20	12	8
Patient 24	20	20	0
Total	480	465	15

Figure 14.2 Shows a data collection spreadsheet comparing the amount of time scheduled for each visit to the provider's work cycle time. In this case Provider J. Doe books one uniform time duration though heavily favors adding longer appointments at the top of the hour, followed by quicker acute appointments. The bias calculated shows the difference between what was planned and what actually occurred for each patient. In some cases it varied by up to 10 minutes though the overall daily total only varied by 15 minutes, or less than a minute per appointment on average.

When the overall daily difference significantly departs from the amount of time planned, then a clinic should consider adjusting the time duration scheduled for appointments, find ways to reduce that difference by improving the workflow, and consider altering the schedule template to include a different mix of appointments. For example, it may seem insignificant if a provider under-schedules each appointment by five minutes, but that difference over 24 appointments in one day creates a two hour daily difference – that is two hours behind schedule or an indication of a provider chronically running behind. If a provider chronically runs ahead of time by two hours, then that is two hours of unused provider capacity to be reclaimed.

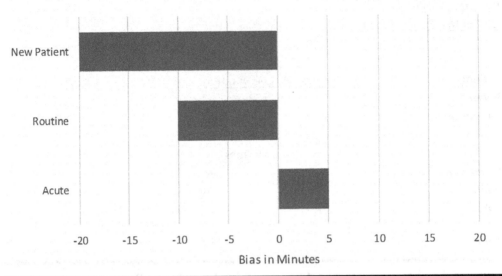

Bias Chart: Provider Cycle Time v. Time Scheduled

Figure 14.3 Identifies the bias in minutes that are booked for each appointment type for each provider. In the example, acute appointments under book time by 5 minutes while routine and New Patient appointments are booked too much time by 20 and 10 minutes respectively. Depending on the mix and number of visits in a given day, there may be an overall difference that indicates whether the provider is on average on time or not.

Day of the Week: Monday			
Provider: J. Doe			
	Number of Appointments		
Appointment Type	**Scheduled**	**Bias**	**Total Bias**
Acute	8	-5	-40
Routine	8	10	80
New Patient	2	20	40
	Total Surplus or Shortage Minutes		**80**

Figure 14.4 Shows how bias impacts a daily scheduled filled with multiple appointments. In the example, there is an average or expected surplus of 80 minutes. While acute appointments are under booked time by 40 minutes, routine and New Patient appointments are allotted too much time. This Monday schedule plans 80 minutes of downtime that with scheduling improvements can be reduced. Further, in order to reduce complexity, acute appointment durations and routine appointment durations could be simplified to the same time of 20 minutes each.

Chapter 15

Questions to Understand how the Provider is the Capacity Constraint

What is the Typical Amount of Time a Provider Spends per Patient Visit?

Along with learning how each provider's true work cycle time for each appointment type compares to what was planned, learning what a provider's general overall average cycle time is will help identify a provider's capacity. One way to do this is by using the cycle time data collected to determine schedule bias. Using the weighted average formula, an overall average cycle time can be calculated with the cycle time per each appointment time and the visit volume for each appointment type. This method is simple but requires someone or a system to collect enough data on actual cycle times. This method also requires a user to make assumptions on the mixture of appointment types and whether those will remain or change. Though it has drawbacks, this method can be the most accurate in terms of true cycle time performance.

If a clinic does not have actual cycle time data, then it can still estimate an average cycle time through other mathematical methods. In this method you take the total hours or minutes a provider was scheduled to see patients and divide it by the total number of patient visits a provider had in a given year. For organizations that can retrieve the amount of scheduled patient care hours per provider and patient visits from an EMR, this method is

Cycle Time: Overall Provider: J. Doe		
Appointment	**Cycle Time (m)**	**Annual Volume**
New	36	250
Routine	16	1,500
Acute	13	500
	Total	**2,250**
Average Cycle Time (m)	17.6	

Figure 15.1   Shows a weighted average method to estimate a provider's overall average cycle time using actual cycle time data per appointment and actual visit volumes. In this case, J. Doe has an overall average cycle time of 17.6 minutes for the 2,250 appointments seen last year. If the volumes of each type of appointment changes, then so does the average cycle time.

quick. The drawback is that hours scheduled for patient care can be off. For example, a provider that runs chronically behind every day scheduled eight hours per day to see patients, but in reality is seeing patients for nine to ten hours per day. The accounting method would base the cycle time on the eight hour day and not what is actually occurring.

Accounting for Average Cycle Time			
	Annual Hours Scheduled	**Annual Visits**	**Average Cycle Time (m)**
D. Jones	1,728	3,500	29.6
J. Doe	1,584	3,301	28.8
W. Smith	1,440	4,001	21.6
A. Thomas	1,440	3,896	22.2
L. King	1,512	4,102	22.1

Figure 15.2   Shows a managerial accounting method identify average cycle times for each provider. Though D. Jones spends the most time in clinic, D. Jones sees the second fewest patients because of the slowest cycle time. This method is simple to calculate but does not account for some of the provider lost time due to patient no shows or the extra time a provider may work if a provider is chronically behind schedule.

Option	Cycle Time (m)	Description of the Method
1	28.2	Total Number of Minutes Available to Schedule Patient Visits per Year Divided by the Number of Visits per Year
2	25.1	Total Number of Minutes Available to Schedule Patient Visits per Year less Time Lost due to Patient No Shows and Unbooked Time Divided by the Number of Visits per Year
3	21.0	During Clinic Cycle Time (see Ch. 10)
4	18.0	Exam Room Cycle Time (see Ch. 10)

Figure 15.3 Shows four different ways to come up with cycle time estimates. Option 1 accounts for provider downtime due to patients not showing or open times in the schedule. Option 2 removes the down time from the equation which makes the estimate closer to a true cycle time. Option 3 is collected through observation or extensive systems but is closer to a true cycle time. Option 4 only includes the time a provider is in the exam room with a patient so does not capture the full work cycle time per patient.

There are a variety of ways to technically calculate a provider overall average cycle time. Each one poses some unique trade-offs and each one requires information from different sources. The best method to use is the one that an organization can calculate fairly easily and which gets team buy-in when it's used.

We calculate a provider's cycle time because a provider is the capacity constraint of the system. From a process perspective, a capacity constraint is the work process that takes the most time. Because the capacity constraint is the most time-consuming step, it is the rate-limiting step or step that determines throughput over a given time period. In clinics, the provider's exam process takes the most time, with occasional exceptions; therefore, throughput is based on a provider's capacity (see Figure 15.4 on page 108).

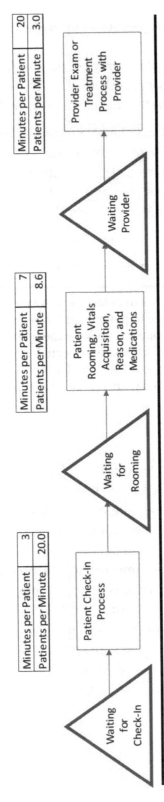

Minutes per Patient	3
Patients per Minute	20.0

Patient Check-In Process

Waiting for Check-In

Minutes per Patient	7
Patients per Minute	8.6

Patient Rooming, Vitals Acquisition, Reason, and Medications

Waiting for Rooming

Minutes per Patient	20
Patients per Minute	3.0

Provider Exam or Treatment Process with Provider

Waiting Provider

Figure 15.4 Shows the application of cycle times in a flow map. The provider process is the capacity constraint to flow because the process takes the longest in the series of work or fewer patients are seen in the same time frame.

How Often do a Provider's Patients Visit?

Providers have patients that will visit the clinic every couple of years, every 18 months, once a year, twice a year, monthly, or more. Patients have different health needs and are in various stages of wellness. Learning how often patients visit a particular provider or clinic in a given year or given 18 months is helpful in understanding the needs of the patient demographics and, to some extent, the practice patterns of the provider, and will help define a provider's capacity. In organizations with electronic medical records, the process to calculate visits per patient is pretty easy. In electronic records there is a history of all visit records so a user can usually select records from a key date-time range and aggregate by each patient account to total the visits.

How Often or How Many Hours a Year does a Provider See Patients?

Providers work many hours a year by plan and by necessity because patients need care. Depending on the provider specialty, provider age, and other personal factors, each provider may work a different number of hours over the course of the year. Each provider may have very different daily schedules, weekly schedules, vacation plans, and holiday plans. In scheduled clinics, the number of hours templated can be extracted from the EMR. If the EMR is not a good option, then a user can extrapolate the daily, weekly, or monthly provider schedule out over the course of a year while accounting for some holidays and vacations.

What is a Provider's Expected Capacity or Panel Size?

A provider's capacity can be expressed as the expected total number of patient visits per year a provider can manage or the expected number of patients per year (or 18 months) a provider can manage. Another name for the expected number of patients a provider can manage is expected Panel Size.

A provider's expected total number of visits per year is derived from the number of hours worked per year and the number of patient visits that can be completed per hour. To convert the capacity measure to patient panel size, take the expected total number of visits per year and divide it by the average number of visits a patient completes per year.

Provider Capacity	
Annual Patient Care Scheduled Hours	1,560
Number of Patients Seen Per Hour (1/Cycle Time)	2.8
Expected Visit Capacity per Year	4,368
Average Number of Visits per Year per Patient	2.5
Expected Panel Size or Provider Capacity (Patients)	1,747

Figure 15.5 Breaks down a provider's expected capacity per year. In the example, the provider should see 4,368 visits per year or manage care for roughly 1,747 patients based on hours scheduled to see patients, a provider's cycle time, and the average number of visits per year per patient.

What is a Provider's Actual Throughput and Panel Size?

Actual patient throughput is simply the number of actual patient visits a provider managed in a year or 18 months. The actual panel size is the number and list of patients a provider managed over a one year or 18 month period. Some EMRs provide panel size estimates; otherwise, it is an electronic assignment process like using the four-cut method or other similar methods to assign patients to panels in order to derive panel size.

Comparing expected to actual performance will identify losses or increases to expected capacity. The actual throughput may differ from expected for a number of reasons, including differences in a) the annual patient care hours b) the provider Cycle time, and c) the average number of visits per patient.

How Many Hours do Providers Work Compared to What is Planned?

Many times, following an assessment of planned capacity and actual output, a large source of a shortage is that fewer hours were worked than what was planned. Providers have lives too. Sometimes a gap emerges when a provider takes more vacation time than expected or drops work to half days on Friday in order to reduce burnout. Other times though, providers get pulled into administrative duties that consume an hour or two, or more, in a week instead of seeing patients. The unplanned administrative hours can add up over the course of a year to dramatically reduce throughput.

Provider Capacity: Actual v. Planned			
	Expected	Actual	% Difference
Annual Patient Care Scheduled Hours	1,560	1,564	0.3%
Number of Patients Seen Per Hour (1/Cycle Time)	2.8	2.8	0.0%
Visit Capacity per Year	4,368	4,380	0.3%
Average Number of Visits per Year per Patient	2.5	2.4	-4.0%
Panel Size or Provider Capacity (Patients)	1,747	1,825	4.5%

Figure 15.6   Shows the actual capacity and throughput of a provider compared to what was planned. In the example, the provider's visit throughput slightly increased because the provider worked slightly more hours than expected while the panel size was much higher due to each patient visiting fewer times per year.

Change in Provider Throughput				
Hours Scheduled	**Throughput**	**Visit Capacity**	**Visits per Patient**	**Total Panel Size**
J. Doe	1,560	2.6	4,056	2.6	1,560
J. Doe	1,560	*2.9*	4,462	2.6	1,716
		Change	406		156
		Percent Change	10.0%		10.0%

Hours Scheduled	**Throughput**	**Visit Capacity**	**Visits per Patient**	**Total Panel Size**
J. Doe	1,560	2.6	4,056	2.6	1,560
J. Doe	*1,404*	2.6	3,650	2.6	1,404
		Change	-406		-156
		Percent Change	-10.0%		-10.0%

Hours Scheduled	**Throughput**	**Visit Capacity**	**Visits per Patient**	**Total Panel Size**
J. Doe	1,560	2.6	4,056	2.6	1,560
J. Doe	*1,404*	*2.9*	4,015	2.6	1,544
		Change	-41		-16
		Percent Change	-1.0%		-1.0%

Figure 15.7 Shows the potential change in a provider's annual visit capacity and panel size. The table at the top shows that J. Doe sped up throughput or visits per hour from 2.6 to 2.9, resulting in a 10% increase. The table in the middle shows that J. Doe reduced the number of annual hours seeing patients by 156 hours resulting in a 10% decline. The table at the bottom shows the combined impact of increasing throughput from 2.6 to 2.9 while dropping 156 hours of patient care – a net 1% loss in annual visits and panel size.

Chapter 16

Questions to Understand the Total Provider Capacity

Are "Extenders" Used?

Physician assistants and nurse practitioners often work as providers, managing a practice of their own patients and visits. Physician assistants and nurse practitioners also work as extenders for a physician. Extenders practice with a physician in order to extend or increase a physician's capacity to see and manage more patients. There are different ways physicians and their extenders may operate together. Some physician extender teams divide patient care equally between them and may literally have patients alternate subsequent visits between each provider. In this method, both provider and extender remain equally engaged with all patients. In other models, extenders might be assigned the responsibility to manage care for the patients with Same Day acute needs, physicals and basic routine follow-up care while the physician manages New Patient visits and more complex follow-up care.

Because the provider is no longer practicing solo, estimating physician extender team capacity is slightly different but still simple to do. To understand the expected and actual capacity for a physician extender team, aggregate the hours worked, visits per year, cycle times, and average visits per patient per year.

Provider Capacity: Physician + Extender Team			
	Physician	Extender	Team Total
Annual Patient Care Scheduled Hours	1,560	1,600	
Number of Patients Seen Per Hour (1/Cycle Time)	2.8	2.6	
Visit Capacity per Year	4,368	4,160	8,528
Average Number of Visits per Year per Patient			2.6
Panel Size or Provider Capacity (Patients)			3,280

Figure 16.1   Breaks down the annual capacity for a physician with extender team. Based on each provider's cycle time and hours scheduled, the two have a capacity for 8,528 visits and panel size of 3,280 patients. Visits per patient per year are based on patients seeing either the physician or the extender.

What is the Combined Panel Size for all Providers?

While there are some clinics that operate with one solo physician or a single physician extender team, more clinics tend to have many providers. To assess the performance and capacity for a group of providers, simply aggregate the hours worked, visits per year, cycle times, and average visits per patient per year the same as you do for individual providers and provider extender teams.

Learning the total capacity for all providers in a group or geographic region is useful in identifying gaps when comparing capacity to the patient population of that demographic region. In some regions or markets, there may be more providers than patients seeking care for a particular specialty. More often, the provider capacity will be only a fraction of the patient population for a given market. Learning the total provider capacity will help identify what proportion of the population can be served or what proportion of a patient market can be captured.

Total Practice Expected Capacity

	Hours Scheduled	Throughput	Visit Capacity	Average Visits per Patient per Year	Total Panel Size
J. Doe	1,560	2.6	4,056		
A. Thomas	1,450	2.8	4,060		
L. King	1,500	2.4	3,600		
W. Smith	1,560	2.9	4,524		
D. Jones	1,200	2.3	2,760		
K. Lee	1,400	2.5	3,500		
P. Singh	1,500	2.7	4,050		
S. Leary	1,560	2.2	3,432		
Total Practice			29,982	2.6	11,532

Figure 16.2   Illustrates a way to calculate the expected visit capacity for an entire practice and total number of patients managed. In this example, providers support other providers in patient care. For example, a patient may be assigned to W. Smith's panel, but has seen J. Doe for Same Day needs when W. Smith was not available. For this reason, the average visits per patient per year were aggregated for all providers rather than for each one, which then produced the 11,532 patients managed by all providers in the clinic.

Chapter 17

Questions to Understand how Physical Space is Used and Managed

Who Preps Point of Care Space and Maintains the Rooms?

Point of care space is where care takes place and it is desirable to make the patient experience in the point of care space as satisfying as possible. A room that is not clean is a dissatisfier. Delay in care due to missing supplies or equipment is frustrating. Clinics use various methods to keep rooms stocked properly and may use different staff members to own the rooms. In unfortunate situations, there may be no methods or no owners.

In one clinic, the MA assigned to support provider J. Doe will own the exam rooms for J. Doe that day. In the morning, before patients arrive, the MA might check that all common use supplies are in the room in the right quantity and check that special use supplies are ready on a cart outside the exam rooms. In the morning and between each patient visit, the MA will do a wipe down turnover of the exam room to make sure it is clean and might do a more thorough clean at the end of the day. In this model, room preparation follows the team using the rooms which creates some ownership. In certain cases though, it can create some standardization challenges if each team does it differently.

In another clinic, MAs might be permanently assigned a series of rooms to maintain. Regardless of which rooms the MA is rooming patients in during the day, the MA prepares the rooms in the morning before the first patient arrives. In other clinics, each MA might be responsible for cleaning the rooms his or her provider is assigned that day, though one designated MA who comes in early ensures all rooms and supplies are in order to a specific standard. There might even be an MA who stays late just to do a more thorough clean of the exam rooms after patients have left. There are various options to accomplishing the same purpose, though each option may bring different trade-offs between flexibility, ownership, standardization, and quality. The key point to learn is whether the room preparation process is efficient and effective so as to not disrupt flow during patient care.

How Flexible are Patient Care Rooms?

Patient care rooms are often designed for one specific care service or one type of physician specialist. A patient care room, especially an exam room with a specific design, provides a focused usability for its user in order to increase efficiency and effectiveness. Very specific designs make sense if a clinic room will be used by only one service or specialty for the foreseeable future or the specialty requires a very specialized room. Unfortunately, inflexible rooms tend to become a poorly utilized high cost space and the more restrictive an organization's patient care rooms are, generally the more rooms are needed overall.

Sometimes a clinic may have mostly exam rooms that are very flexible in use, but then there are one or two exam rooms or procedure rooms that fit only one purpose. For example, a clinic may have a room with a procedure chair, stocked with procedure supplies. While the room was intended to be the place to complete procedures, the procedures are commonly completed in the other exam rooms making the room mostly useless other than for storage. Perhaps a clinic has mostly exam rooms that are flexibly used except for one or two that are shaped oddly because of the building design, or are located much further away from the rest of the rooms so the care team rarely uses them.

On the other hand, clinics using universal and flexible space can maximize the utilization of that space. A flexible space is designed to allow different services or provider specialties to use the same space. Flexible space is often interchangeable for provider teams during a given clinic hour, clinic day, or day of the week, so that there is little room downtime as long as there are providers needing space to work. Further, rooms constructed

Type of Space	Specific Space	Quantity	Comments
Point of Care Space	Exam Rooms	18	Multi use Exam Rooms
Point of Care Space	Exam Rooms	4	Smaller End rooms seldom used due to space and distance
Point of Care Space	Lab/Collection	1	Blood draw stations
Point of Care Space	Procedure Room	1	Procedures done in Exam Rooms, used as storage
	Total	24	
	Flexible	*18*	
	% Flexible	*75%*	

Figure 17.1 Shows a point of care room inventory. In this clinic there are 18 multi-use flexible exam rooms and four seldom used exam rooms because of the design of the rooms and location. Further, the procedure room in the clinic is seldom used. Excluding the lab draw station, only 75% of the point of care space is used flexibly.

without fixed cabinetry, fixed tables, and stationary devices are generally flexible for future changes; as change frequently occurs in healthcare, flexibility to change is generally positive.

How are Rooms Allocated to Providers?

Regardless of whether a room is flexible or has restricted use, there is typically some general allocation of rooms to a provider during a clinic day. The number of rooms available and allocated to a provider can increase a provider's productivity up to a point before the issued rooms become an excess. Room allocation is an optimization challenge because you want to get the most out of each individual provider's productivity without creating surplus costs or without reducing the total number of providers that can work in the same space for an overall high total provider productivity.

The number of rooms a provider needs can be based off some basic time measures: a) the amount of time a provider sees patients in the patient care space b) the amount of time other clinical support staff need to see patients in the patient care space c) any time needed for a patient to get prepped for an exam or procedure d) any holding time a provider needs to keep patients in the patient care room while still working on that patient and e) the amount of time a provider is scheduled to see a patient. Room need ideally does not include the amount of time patients have to wait in the exam room or other downtime, though some organizations include it.

How organizations assign rooms can further impact how rooms are allocated and subsequent utilization of the space. For instance, one clinic may permanently assign exam rooms 1–3 to Provider A. Thomas even though A. Thomas only works three and a half days in the clinic. For the rest of the week, those rooms sit idle. Another clinic may assign A. Thomas three exam rooms each day that A. Thomas is working so that the rooms do not sit idle the rest of the week. Then a third clinic knows that A. Thomas needs more than two exam rooms to see patients but likely not three full exam rooms over the course of a day. Because the clinic design pools a group of exam rooms together, the clinic dynamically assigns rooms to each provider based on need throughout the day. Basically, each provider is alerted to which room the next patient is in as the provider moves to that next patient. By dynamically assigning rooms, the clinic avoids over issuing or under issuing rooms.

Room Allocation First Level Planning

	1	1.5	2	2.5	3	3.5	4
Exam Rooms Allocated							
Average Scheduled Visit Cycle Time	20						
Time Needed in the Exam Room per Visit							
Provider	18						
Provider Time Buffer	6						
Other Staff	10						
Other Staff Time Buffer	7						
Total	41						
Room Surplus / Deficit Time	-21						
Adjusted Room Surplus / Deficit Time	-21	-11	-1	9	19	29	39

Figure 17.2 Shows a simple first level room allocation planning table that indicates a provider needs over two exam rooms to manage patient flow. The calculations account for the amount of time visits are scheduled for and the time needed to work in the exam room by the provider and staff. This model also allows for real world buffer times or variation allowances. The "Room Surplus/Deficit Time" indicates if there is enough scheduled time to complete the work in the one exam. The "Adjusted Room Surplus/Deficit Time" includes the number of rooms allocated to identify the point at which, theoretically, there are enough rooms to complete the work.

What is the Utilization of Patient Care Space?

Utilization of patient care space is measured as the amount of time patient care space is used by patients compared to the amount of time the space is available. It is better not to include the time patients are simply waiting in the patient care room in the utilization measure. Though it can get tricky to discount that information when measuring, doing observation studies or using other technical systems, it is possible to do so.

In clinics, patient care space should be used to increase each provider's productivity without reducing the productivity for all providers or without creating a heavily under-utilized space. For example, if one provider is only assigned one room and spends 20 minutes with each patient while her staff spend 15 minutes with each patient in the exam room and only 5 minutes getting the next patient, then over the course of a day, the utilization of that room would be over 87%. Unfortunately, because there is only one room, the provider will be waiting 20 minutes for every 20 minutes spent with a patient so she will be utilized 50% of the day. In reality, a clinic wants providers utilized as close to 100% as possible so room utilization will typically be much lower to accommodate this goal.

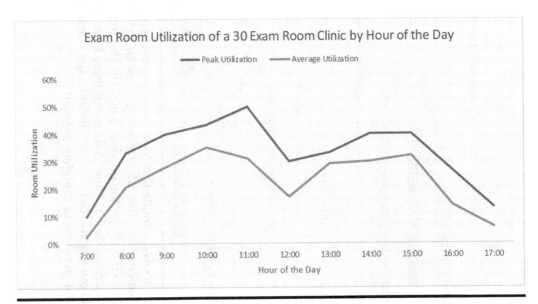

Figure 17.3 **Charts the peak and average exam room utilization for 10 working hours of the clinic day. The chart shows the typical "M" shape of a traditional clinic with morning and afternoon sessions with a lunch break. At its busiest, 11am, the example clinic was using 15 out of 30 exam rooms, which is not uncommon.**

Total Practice Expected Capacity (24 Exam Rooms)

	Weekly Throughput	Hours Scheduled Weekly	Patients / Hour	Open Hours	Open Room Hours
J. Doe	88	34	2.6	6	18
A. Thomas	90	32	2.8	8	24
L. King	77	32	2.4	8	24
W. Smith	99	34	2.9	6	18
D. Jones	55	24	2.3	16	48
K. Lee	75	30	2.5	10	30
P. Singh	86	32	2.7	8	24
S. Leary	75	34	2.2	6	18
TOTAL	**645**	**252**	**2.6**	**68**	**204**
		Additional Visit Potential		173	
		Percent Increase		27%	

Figure 17.4   Is a summary table of an eight provider 24 exam room practice. In this practice, each provider works from three exam rooms, but no provider works full hours each work week; therefore, there is surplus exam room space that could accommodate 68 more hours of provider time. If there is no need or want for additional providers to work in that space, then the exam rooms will sit idle. If there is a need or want, then filling the open hours up with providers that on average work at the average pace of the existing eight providers means a 27% increase in weekly visits.

What is the Potential for any Underutilized Space?

Exam rooms often sit idle depending on the time of day or day of the week. Obviously, every night after working hours, all exam rooms sit idle, but frequently exam rooms are not used during the working day for various reasons. Though an exam room alone does not see or care for patients, knowing the number of open exam room hours can identify potential capacity increases should that need or want arise.

The same is true for underutilized space even though under-utilized space is harder to identify than open space. For example, an Internal Medicine clinic has 18 exam rooms and staffs six providers each weekday to care for patients. It was decided, without evidence, that each provider should have three exam rooms permanently assigned. Each provider spends a great deal of time with each patient, typically 30–60 minutes, while staff spend usually only 5–15 minutes with each patient in the exam room. In this example, the providers do not need more than two exam rooms so there is an excess of six rooms which is enough to accommodate three more providers with two exam rooms each.

It is important to note, that not every provider works at the same pace, especially if we are discussing providers from different specialties, though it is common to see providers of the same specialty working at very different rates too. Because providers work at different paces and require different amounts of time seeing patients in the exam room, it makes sense to offer different room allocations for each provider. When actively searching or deciding on which providers to recruit or add to a clinic schedule because there is excess space, the room allocation factor can help determine if providers "fit", but typically revenues, costs, and other factors are necessary to create a better business case.

Potential Extra Capacity and Throughput (2.0 pts/hour and average reimbursement $101 per Visit)						
	Rooms Open	2 Room Providers	Hours Open	Open Room Hours	Provider Hours	Visit Potential	Revenue Potential
Monday	2	1	8	16.0	8	16 $	1,616
Tuesday	3	1	10	30.0	10	20 $	2,020
Wednesday	2	1	6	12.0	6	12 $	1,212
Thursday	3	1	8	24.0	8	16 $	1,616
Friday	6	3	10	60.0	30	60 $	6,060
TOTAL	16		42	142.0	62	124 $	12,524

Potential Extra Capacity and Throughput (3.0 pts/hour and average reimbursement $90 per Visit)						
	Rooms Open	3 Room Providers	Hours Open	Open Room Hours	Provider Hours	Visit Potential	Revenue Potential
Monday	2	0	8	16.0	0	0 $	-
Tuesday	3	1	10	30.0	10	30 $	2,700
Wednesday	2	0	6	12.0	0	0 $	-
Thursday	3	1	8	24.0	8	24 $	2,160
Friday	6	2	10	60.0	20	60 $	5,400
TOTAL	16		42	142.0	38	114 $	10,260

Figure 17.5   Is a summary table showing open exam rooms by day of the week with the associated hours the rooms are open. The table at the top shows how many providers that work at a two patient per hour pace can fit in the space available while the bottom identifies how many providers working at a three patients per hour pace ideally fit. Monday and Wednesday are not ideal for providers working at a busier three patient per hour pace because there are not enough rooms, though Tuesday and Thursday are better suited. Fridays could be staffed by two faster or three slower providers, though if extending to review revenues, the providers seeing two patients per hour may be worth it. There are plenty of other factors to consider, but these are the basics.

Chapter 18

Questions to Understand the Equipment and Technology Used

What Electronic Registration Systems are Used?

There are numerous electronic systems to support healthcare processes and numerous sub-systems within each electronic system. Some electronic systems integrate well with other systems, while some do not, which can make a process clunky. Some electronic systems have a broad spectrum suite of solutions that cover almost all the needs of a clinic while other systems are very focused and niche. Electronic systems are some of the biggest tools staff and providers use, for better or worse, in patient care clinics. Learning what electronic systems exist and how well the systems are implemented can explain a great deal about a clinic's efficiency and even staff satisfaction.

Electronic systems used at registration may or may not be part of the EMR suite. Many integrated EMR systems connect the clinical documentation with the registration process to simplify billing and check-in processes. Other times, the check-in system is a separate component like a stand-alone patient scheduling system. The electronic system for credit card co-payment processing may be another stand-alone system, as might the electronic signature capture software. Electronic forms are becoming a normal part of EMR suites but may still require a separate module of the EMR suite to be purchased. Kiosks or mobile devices for check-in applications may be stand-alone or perhaps display a module attached to the EMR.

Good electronic systems at registration are well integrated and make the check-in and registration process more efficient, flexible, and more effective. The trade-off is often that better systems tend to have a heavier initial price tag, but not always.

What Electronic Clinical Documentation Systems are Used?

Providers and clinical support staff spend a large percentage of time working in the clinical documentation system. The system of records is where patient care notes are entered, patient information is retrieved, messages are sent or received, and more. Once staff and providers are comfortable with a specific system, it is difficult to change to another system so system change happens infrequently. Optimization, updates, and modifications to the documentation system are more common and may occur routinely.

Documentation systems come in various forms, costs, levels of integration, and more. One system may be designed for easier data entry and display of information. Another system may be designed to retrieve patient information more easily or to complete aggregated analysis of patients better. Understanding which documentation system is deployed and the electronic systems trade-offs will often identify why clinic staff work the way they work and explain why staff may be dissatisfied.

What System is Used for Scheduling?

Patient appointment scheduling systems may be a module connected to the EMR or a stand-alone system. Patient scheduling systems can aid or hinder a clinic's ability to manage provider capacity, throughput, and access. Good scheduling systems allow managers to easily modify provider templates, appointment durations, and the times providers work. Good scheduling systems make it easy for schedulers to create appointments without extraneous searching. A good scheduling system matched to the registration system and EMR makes it easy to run analysis on lead times, No Shows, throughput, provider capacity, and capacity utilization.

What Diagnostic and Clinic Equipment is Used?

Clinics use a host of diagnostic and medical equipment like weight scales, height bars, blood pressure devices, exam tables, temperature probes, pulse oximeters, spirometry equipment, and more. There are usually very low or no tech options to the equipment and much more high-tech options for the same equipment. The low-tech options are affordable and are tried and true for clinics. The low-tech manual options work but can create extra work and transcription steps for staff which potentially increase risks of error. Higher end options use technology to its fullest by automating work steps, integrating with EMRs to remove transcription steps, and targeting patient satisfaction. Higher end options cost generally more up front but have potential to reduce costs long term depending on the device and how well the device was designed.

How is Technology Used?

Technology can be a great aid and amplifier for great staff, processes, clinic designs, and equipment though it can be the complete opposite if not integrated well. Each time new technology is incorporated into a clinic, that technology creates trade-offs. Some of the trade-offs are known ahead of time while others tend to surprise clinic staff. Good technology and implementations augment good processes, staff, and clinic designs. The trade-offs are acceptable to the users and the overall processes and performance improve with good technology or implementations. Bad technology and implementations tend to surprise staff with unacceptable trade-offs and decrease the efficiency of an existing process or overall clinic performance.

Many clinics do not complete enough due diligence before purchase and some even favor a disconnected haphazard approach to technology acquisition. Technology acquisition decisions tend to be driven differently in different organizations and might be based on factors that include a desire for organizational standardization, an administrator's quest for more insights, or one provider's preference. Some organizations will have a formal process for acquisition while others are less structured. It is helpful to learn what the acquisition drivers and processes are as well as how well technology is implemented.

KEY INFRASTRUCTURE CONCEPTS

Chapter 19

Questions to Understand Leadership and Management Systems

Who are the Formal Leaders in the Clinic or Practice?

All managers and supervisors in a clinic are formal leaders because of their title or position. All providers are also formal leaders in a clinic because of their role in leading patient care. How strong and aligned the formal leaders in a clinic are often makes or breaks a clinic's performance. Having buy-in from the formal leaders carries great weight in making changes to the clinic, whether through process change, purchasing new equipment, trialing new technology, or redesigning the physical space. Very few clinic initiatives will succeed without some level of buy-in and alignment from the core formal leadership team in a clinic.

Who are the Informal Leaders in the Practice or Clinic?

While all managers should be leaders, not all leaders are managers or formal leaders. Humans lead one another through influence. Informal leaders in an organization tend to lead by providing others with direction, especially when clear direction is not coming from formal leaders or if the direction

Inventory of Clinic Leaders

Formal Leaders	Role	Alignment Notes
W. Collins	West Region Medical Director	Has a focus on technology innovation
R. Pierce	West Region Practice Director	Not very involved with the practices
D. Jones, MD	Medical Director	Follows W. Collins's ideas
Z. Barnes	Practice Manager	Has a focus on Front Office priorities mostly
E. Lloyd	Front Office Supervisor	Not very involved
S. Norman, CMA	Clinical Supervisor	Influenced by J. Doe
J. Doe, MD	Provider - PCP	Disagrees with D. Jones and Z. Barnes on direction
W. Smith, DO	Provider - PCP	Meets own goals and does not get involved
A. Thomas, PA	Provider - PCP	Follows J. Doe
L. King, CNP	Provider - PCP	Meets own goals and does not get involved

Informal Leaders	Role	Alignment Notes
R. Green, CMA	J. Doe's MA	Influences staff with J. Doe's ideas
B. Browne	Receptionist	Great influencer for improved patient experience

Figure 19.1 Shows an inventory of the various leaders of a specific clinic along with some simple notes on how everyone is aligned with others. The inventory begins with the two external leaders of the clinic, followed by the administrators within the clinic, and then each provider. Key informal leaders are also included because the two hold influence over other staff. The inventory is a simple way to note the leadership structure of a clinic.

from the informal leader sounds better. Informal leaders tend to supply others with the reason why things should or should not be done and especially fill in when formal leaders do not convey this purpose. Informal leaders tend to know how to motivate those others around them and frequently do so. Informal leaders in an organization may act completely in alignment with the formal leaders so that these informal leaders truly enforce leadership. Informal leaders may arise because formal leaders are not leading. Informal leaders may act completely opposite to the formal leaders in the manner of sabotage. Informal leaders in a clinic might be one outspoken medical assistant or one unhappy scheduler. While informal leaders hold no budgetary power or formal authority, they can also make or break any clinic performance initiative by influencing those around them.

How is the Practice Managed?

Clinic managers have different styles and competencies. Clinics have unique cultures and working climates. Clinics can be top-down controlled by management where decisions and information are disseminated from top managers. Clinics can be bottom-up driven where best practices and decisions are floated up from engaged staff to management that act as coaches. Clinics can have a mix of both top-down and bottom-up management aspects. In clinics, good managers tend to lead, complete, or participate heavily in organizational planning, organizing how to accomplish work, staffing people to accomplish the work, leading people and implementing controls or feedback to stay on course.

Managerial planning includes annual budget planning, business planning for a clinic, planning for performance improvement, or is a specific task a manager does in planning. For instance, a practice manager planning costs for the next year, may collect demand projections from market data, may include provider cycle times, may include total provider capacity, and may include benchmarks on staff expenses per providers in order to arrive at a specific budgetary cost number expressed as a planned number of staff needed. Some managers have very analytical planning processes while others may be less precise and others may even be rather haphazard. While planning occurs at any time, most planning tends to occur around budget cycles, new facility design or redesign, or capital equipment purchases.

Organizing how work gets accomplished involves establishing work in workflows or processes, grouping resources into teams, and establishing priorities for the team. It refers to the organizational hierarchies or structures deployed by the manager to his or her group. Some clinics may have very specific processes, workflows, team structures, and hierarchies, while others do not. It is not uncommon for clinics to have few defined processes and very little formal team organization around getting work done. As clinics are often based around how individual providers work, a clinic may act as a collection of self-directed provider teams. Organizing tends to occur when something changes or the group is undergoing some form of reorganization like significantly changing work processes, adding in new workflows for additional providers, or changing teams for new care models.

Clinic staffing by managers involves acquiring and allocating resources for teams and providers daily, weekly, monthly, and long term. An ideal manager's goal with staffing is to make sure resources match demand without excess costs, but it could be based on satisfying what a provider wants too. Clinic managers may be busy each day working with staff that call out, hiring new staff, creating next month's work schedule, or physically having to step in and work as a staff member. Work around staffing seems never to end and is a continuous effort.

Managers are in a position of authority and hold natural influence over staff. Some clinic managers rest with authority while other managers work to truly lead a clinic team to accomplish exceptional work. As stated before, humans lead one another through influence. Leaders in an organization tend to lead by providing others with specific and overall direction. Leaders tend to supply others with the reason why things will or will not be done. Leaders tend to know how to motivate and will deliberately motivate staff in various ways to accomplish work that meets a specific standard or goal. Managerial leadership is a continuous process that formal leaders exert, though in some cases, managers may display a lack of leadership.

Controls and feedback deployed by managers involve deploying an awareness component and an action component. In order to control the clinic processes, managers must be aware of certain results or activities. With this awareness, the clinic manager can act or have processes that act for the manager in response to the clinic results or activities. For example, a clinic manager should know which staff are late or stay late and how often they do so, so that reward, discipline, or discussions can occur to reach the desired outcome. Clinic managers should know if costs exceed

Staff	Meeting	Frequency	Purpose
Providers	Clinical Huddle	Daily	Internal Clinic communication meeting to review pertinent information for today's patient care activities between a Provider's Care Team. 2-5 minutes
	All Staff	Monthly	Internal Clinic meeting to review routine administrative, business, clinical, service, and quality information with the team. Discuss any non-routine important clinic wide upcoming impacts. 30-60 minutes
	All Providers	Quarterly	Internal Clinic meeting to discuss Provider related issues, clinic performance, care guidelines, and relevant changes impacting Providers. 30-60 minutes
Staff	Admin Huddle	Daily	Internal Clinic communication meeting to review pertinent information for today's schedule focused on administrative information between Management, Support, and Clinical Staff. 2-5 minutes
	Clinical Huddle	Daily	Internal Clinic communication meeting to review pertinent information for today's patient care activities between a Provider's Care Team. 2-5 minutes
	Performance	Weekly	Internal working huddle to discuss clinic performance issues, continuous improvement ideas, clinic performance relative to the last week's priorities, and next week's focus for improvement work. 10-30 minutes
	All Staff	Monthly	Internal Clinic meeting to review routine administrative, business, clinical, service, and quality information with the team. Discuss any non-routine important clinic wide upcoming impacts. 30-60 minutes
Management	Admin Huddle	Daily	Internal Clinic communication meeting to review pertinent information for today's schedule focused on administrative information between Management, Support, and Clinical Staff. 2-5 minutes
	Leadership Huddle	Daily	External communication meeting between practice leadership and the managers in the next level of the management hierarchy to cover administrative, urgent, and coordinating issues. 5-10 minutes
	Performance	Weekly	Internal working huddle to discuss clinic performance issues, continuous improvement ideas, clinic performance relative to the last week's priorities, and next week's focus for improvement work. 10-30 minutes
	All Staff	Monthly	Internal Clinic meeting to review routine administrative, business, clinical, service, and quality information with the team. Discuss any non-routine important clinic wide upcoming impacts. 30-60 minutes
	Practice Leadership	Monthly	External formal review meeting between practice leadership and the managers in the next level of the management hierarchy to review business performance, clinical performance, and performance towards designated goals and priorities. 30-60 minutes
	All Providers	Quarterly	Internal Clinic meeting to discuss Provider related issues, clinic performance, care guidelines, and relevant changes impacting Providers. 30-60 minutes
	Operations Review	Quarterly	External formal review meeting between practice leadership and the managers in the next two levels of the management hierarchy to review the organization's business performance, clinical performance, and performance towards designated goals and priorities. 60 minutes

Figure 19.2   Is an example table highlighting different communication meetings that each staff member might attend. Each meeting has a slightly different purpose, frequency, and duration. The more frequent meetings are intended to be quicker, but critical to maintaining information flow throughout the clinic team.

revenues by more than planned in order to find out why and then work toward the desired outcome. Ideally, clinic managers should know ahead of time that costs are trending to exceed revenues so that adjustments can be made prior to the exception. Each clinic has different control systems in place but most all have at least some basic form of financial control like a budget, personnel control like human resource policies on staff tardiness, or patient satisfaction control like a patient wait time policy or correction process.

How Often are there All Staff Meetings and All Provider Meetings?

Good communication is a key component to building trust and aligning a clinic. Good communication processes help managers to lead, control, and receive feedback on all other managerial responsibilities. During a given clinic day though, it is a challenge to get all staff and all providers together to disseminate information and receive feedback. Getting all staff and all providers together daily is often unnecessary, though if clinics do not engage in some two-way communication at some periodic frequency, then critical discussions and knowledge sharing are missed. In healthcare systems, change is common, so the communication to all staff and all providers should at least keep up with that rate of change.

How Often are there Team Huddles?

A quick and less manpower intensive way to coordinate and communicate is through daily huddles. A huddle is not intended to last much more than five or ten minutes. Huddles work best in the morning before patient care begins, or mid-day following a lunch break. In clinics there are generally two parts or types of huddles.

The first is the administrative huddle where key information is disseminated to all staff to make the team aware or to elicit quick feedback. Perhaps there is a new vendor coming to the clinic tomorrow, or a new registration technology change beginning today, or management is soliciting feedback on a recent process change. The purpose of the administrative huddle is to disseminate near term information to give all staff a heads up and to receive fresh feedback from them.

The second is the patient care huddle where key information is disseminated and discussed within a patient care team about patients who recently visited or patients who are visiting today or tomorrow. The huddles involve reminding the team about key supplies or equipment needed, instructions for what to do with schedule if extenuating circumstances exist, and open feedback or reminders regarding patient care relevant to the small team.

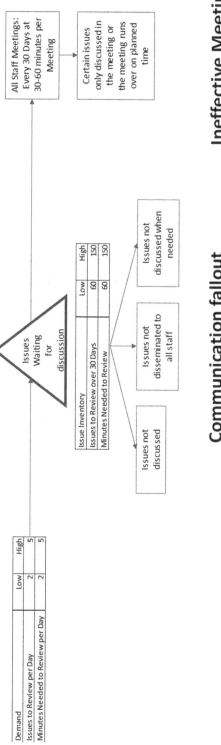

Demand	Low	High
Issues to Review per Day	2	5
Minutes Needed to Review per Day	2	5

Issues not discussed

Issue Inventory	Low	High
Issues to Review over 30 Days	60	150
Minutes Needed to Review	60	150

Issues not disseminated to all staff

Issues not discussed when needed

Issues Waiting for discussion

All Staff Meetings: Every 30 Days at 30-60 minutes per Meeting

Certain issues only discussed in the meeting or the meeting runs over on planned time

Communication fallout   **Ineffective Meeting**

Figure 19.3   Shows a typical communication process where there are no planned daily huddles, daily communication sessions, or daily communication methods. Because of the time sensitivity of some issues and the number of issues accumulated over a 30 day period, communication fallout occurs and eventually the planned monthly meeting is overburdened with topics or does not cover enough.

How Does the Practice Manager Engage with Support Teams?

Unlike manager counterparts in Acute Care settings, clinic managers often do not readily see or even have a strong support team network. Some clinics manage the entire support system alone while others leverage Healthcare system resources. Even with system level support, individual clinics and managers may not receive routine support or a clinic manager may not understand fully what resources are available at the system level to support the clinic or how to access those resources. While there are regular management and support staff rounds in Acute Care settings like hospitals, there is rarely support management rounding through a series of healthcare system clinics.

Because of the physical disconnect from support functions, clinics often take on more work tasks than needed and may or may not complete certain support functions more efficiently or effectively. Learning how practice managers engage and how often they engage with support managers can identify efficiencies in the clinic system.

Are there Management Systems like Lean in Place?

Many healthcare organizations have adopted some form of performance improvement methodology that helps the organization's managers and staff make continuous improvement. The methodologies prescribe ways to engage staff, problem solve, prioritize decisions, and improve continually. The performance improvement methods are really just formal ways for the organization to manage so that each individual or individual manager is not left to decide the best way to manage everything. These organizations have adopted a management system or parts of a management system methodology. Lean, Six Sigma, Agile, Toyota Production System, Plan DO Control Act, and more are all examples of management systems.

In organizational cultures where a managerial system is accepted, the management systems tend to create good results for the organization. The management systems tend to allow managers to spend less time on figuring out how to manage – planning, organizing, controlling, and staffing – and more time leading.

Chapter 20

Questions to Understand the History of the Clinic

Was the Practice Acquired by a Larger Health System?

In the last decade or so, healthcare systems have proactively acquired physician practices in order to capture and better control market share as well as to better coordinate total care between Acute and Ambulatory Care. Many clinics owned by physicians have sold a private practice or group practice to healthcare systems. In other cases, healthcare systems have formed completely new clinics and practices by hiring in providers.

Practices that have been acquired by a healthcare system bring with them a unique culture that may or may not seamlessly fit into the larger healthcare system culture. Provider preferences and productivity goals may not perfectly align with healthcare system goals despite the assumptions made during acquisition. When a practice is assembled by a health system by hiring in providers, the healthcare system has some chance of finding providers that fit the organization's culture or are willing to fit.

Was the Practice Formed from Disparate Provider Practices?

Any clinic may house a practice or practices that formed from individual provider practices or smaller provider group practices. Each individual provider or smaller group practice may have preferences and ideas on how a clinic should run. When combined into a larger group practice or clinic team, there may be team fusion, or the clinic may operate practically as separate entities sharing the same space and resources.

It is generally easier from a management and resourcing standpoint when providers are aligned and practice in a similar manner as it makes processes more consistent. Understanding how providers came to work for the clinic is an indicator of how uniformly the clinic performs.

How Many and Which Providers have been in Private Practice?

Providers that have owned, managed, or been partners in private practices have at least a general idea what it takes to financially keep a clinic running. Private practice physicians must take ownership of the bottom line and take home what is appropriate while keeping the practice afloat. In tough markets, private practice providers remain cost-efficient and maintain satisfied patients in order to attract more patients. Many private practice providers are very entrepreneurial and exploit opportunities. In fact, some have exploited the acquisition process to major healthcare systems to get amazing deals for the practice. While those providers that have only experienced the employee provider status are not sheltered from the business side of running practices, private practice providers tend to have more experience and awareness of the details.

Chapter 21

Questions to Understand the Strategy and Overall Challenges to Consider

What is the Role of the Clinic?

How an organization functions should be in direct alignment with the purpose of that organization. Each clinic should have a purpose why that clinic exists. Of course, clinics exist to supply patient care services to patients, but there can be more refined purpose. A clinic may exist to attract young families into the healthcare system. A clinic may provide convenience care in a specific geographic area in order to increase patient access to basic health care needs for that specific geographic area. A clinic may exist to provide comprehensive care services to patients at or below poverty level for a few specific neighborhoods. A multi-specialty clinic may exist to manage care of high risk elderly patients with various chronic conditions in order to reduce admissions or readmissions to hospitals.

Some organizations are becoming very specific about their target customers and are trying not to be everything to all types of patients. While some organizations take a more proactive and planned approach to defining purpose for a clinic, others let each provider attract the patients that he or she can attract. Generally, clinics with a more refined specific purpose can deploy fewer processes, less complexity, and more uniform strategies. On the other hand, if the purpose is too specific for a given market, then there may not be enough patients to sustain the clinic operation.

What Strategies does the Clinic Deploy and are they Aligned with the Purpose?

Clinic leaders may consciously deploy strategies to differentiate a clinic to its patients. Other clinic leaders may unknowingly use strategies. In either case, in order to understand any strategic shortcomings, it is helpful to know what strategies are deployed and whether those strategies align with the purpose for the clinic. Learning about which strategies and tactics are deployed by a clinic and monitoring the clinic performance will help identify the effectiveness of the strategies.

Clinics deploy strategies and tactics in several ways. Clinics commonly use strategies around location of clinics, strategies on how clinics are laid out, strategies around how care services are designed, strategies on how to price services, strategies around clinic processes, and strategies to differentiate a clinic's quality of care. Some strategies often involve technology innovation, but these can also fit into the process strategies because they are so interconnected.

Clinic	Purpose	Key Strategies	Strategy Deployment and Tactics
Convenience Clinic	Provide convenience care in a specific geographic area in order to increase patient access to basic healthcare needs for that specific geographic area	Location	Clinic is physically located in a convenient location where patients routinely visit for other purposes: a supermarket or corner pharmacy
		Service Design	Clinic provides a limited number of services but those services are routinely needed in the community The Clinic Providers are Certified Nurse Practitioners that perform the care services at the same level of quality as Physicians, but at a better cost
		Pricing	Services are priced more affordably especially for patients with no insurance or high deductible insurance
		Process	The clinic operates a first come first serve model with electronic check in and waiting alerts
Community Clinic	Provide families with greater access to care and attract young families into the healthcare system	Location	Clinic is easily accessible and physically located in the intersection of three neighborhoods with large young family populations Clinic offers teleconference visits with Providers in addition to office visits
		Service Design	Clinic offers weekday early morning and late afternoon same day appointments or walk in visits and Saturday visits
		Process	Clinic assigns a Primary Care Provider to each Family and a Care Team to manage 24/7/365 needs Clinic promotes mobile scheduling, mobile check in, and patients to self room upon arrival
		Layout	Clinic is designed in an "on stage / off stage" manner with family themed corridors for ease of self navigation

Figure 21.1 Breaks down the deployed strategies and tactics for two clinics with different purposes, though the clinics routinely compete against one another for some of the same patients in a geographic area. Strategies and deployment tactics are often shaped due to competition.

Chapter 22

Questions to Understand the Key Measurements

What is the P&L?

The bottom line identifies whether a clinic is losing more money than making or making more than losing. The net earnings, net income, or net profits are all interchangeable ways to explain the bottom line. While net income is important, it is often important to understand how a clinic's net income performs to its budget rather than simple net income.

While ideally any business entity or business unit is profitable, there might be reasons for losses. Some clinics only account for revenues generated within the clinic and not downstream revenues in other parts of a health system. For example, after acquisition, some clinics shed ancillary testing services and the associated revenues to the healthcare system to manage while retaining the same support staff and number of providers. What used to be part of the practice's profit & loss is now recorded elsewhere in the overall organization's income statement, leaving the local clinic statement to show a negative change. In many clinic income statements, it is actually expected to see losses on the bottom line because the downstream revenues generated by the clinic for the health system will show up as profits for the health system bottom line.

What is the Bottom Line per Provider per Year?

Knowing the bottom line is helpful but not always comparable from clinic to clinic or practice to practice. Taking the bottom line and dividing it by the

		Fiscal Year Income / Variance Report		
		Actual	Budget	% Variance
1	Outpatient Revenues	8,365,419	7,457,876	12.2%
2	Revenue Adjustments	(2,541,951)	(1,588,884)	-60.0%
3	Charitable Giving	(7,837)	(3,072)	-155.1%
4	Bad Debt	(180,336)	(192,221)	6.2%
5	Net Patient Revenue	5,635,294	5,673,698	-0.7%
6	Other Operating Income	15,048	7,800	92.9%
7	Net Operating Income	5,650,342	5,681,498	-0.5%
8	Staff Salaries & Wages	823,522	784,047	-5.0%
9	Provider Salaries	2,942,352	2,834,899	-3.8%
10	Employee Benefits	628,236	664,295	5.4%
11	Total Labor Expense	4,394,110	4,283,242	-2.6%
12	Purchased Services	652,685	628,572	-3.8%
13	Supplies	783,336	845,052	7.3%
14	Rental Expense	239,343	284,991	16.0%
15	Utilities	2,652	4,167	36.4%
15	Insurance	31,878	39,750	19.8%
16	Other	63,852	59,976	-6.5%
17	Depreciation	78,818	105,589	25.4%
18	Total Non-Labor Expenses	1,852,564	1,968,098	5.9%
19	Total Expenses	6,246,674	6,251,339	0.1%
20	Net Income	(596,332)	(569,841)	-4.6%

Figure 22.1 Is an income breakdown by revenues and expenses for a 12 month fiscal year. In this clinic, the bottom line or net income is an actual loss of $596,332 as recorded within the clinic which is an unfavorable variation to budget by just under 5%. In the clinic, revenues were lower than expected while labor costs were higher.

number of providers makes the measure more comparable and more useful. In many clinics, there may be two, or three or more providers that work part-time. In order to make the measure meaningful, part-time providers are aggregated up to full-time equivalents. For example, three providers work half time so adding time up comes out to 1.5 provider FTE (0.5+0.5+0.5).

	Net Income per Provider FTE			
		Actual	**Budget**	**% Variance**
5	Net Patient Revenue	5,635,294	5,673,698	-0.7%
7	Net Operating Income	5,650,342	5,681,498	-0.5%
11	Total Labor Expense	4,394,110	4,283,242	-2.6%
18	Total Non-Labor Expenses	1,852,564	1,968,098	5.9%
19	Total Expenses	6,246,674	6,251,339	0.1%
20	Net Income	(596,332)	(569,841)	-4.6%
21	Provider FTE	8	8	0.0%
22	Net Income per Provider FTE	(74,541)	(71,230)	-4.6%

Figure 22.2 Shows the calculation for the average net income per provider FTE in the clinic. In the case above, each provider FTE has a net loss of over $70,000, which may or may not be offset by other revenues created by the provider but realized in other parts of the health system. In many cases, a more precise net income per provider FTE can be calculated for each provider by breaking down revenues earned by each provider and the specific associated costs for each provider.

Ideally there is profit, but often there is loss and that is expected in many clinics because of the larger downstream revenue contributions the provider delivers. The goal is to create a profit or minimize loss so that at the system level there is a profit from the downstream revenues.

How Many Staff FTEs are there per Provider?

In healthcare the largest driver of costs is labor resources. In order to compare the cost driver between providers, practices, and clinics it is helpful to assess the number of full-time equivalent staff that work per provider or full-time equivalent provider. Maintaining the right staff per provider is an optimization challenge because if a clinic has too few resources to support a provider, a provider's capacity to see more patients diminishes. If a provider has too many staff resources, then at some point the staff no longer enhance a provider's capacity to see more patients and become added cost that impacts the bottom line.

		Staff FTE per Provider FTE		
		Actual	Budget	% Variance
21	Provider FTE	8	8	0.0%
22	Staff FTE	26	24.5	-6.1%
23	Staff FTE per Provider FTE	3.3	3.1	-6.1%

Figure 22.3   Shows the simple calculation for the average number of staff FTE per provider FTE. In the example above, the clinic had 3.3 staff FTE per provider FTE which was 0.2 more staff FTE per provider FTE (or 1.6 total FTE = 8′ 0.2) than planned.

What is the Staff Expense per Provider FTE?

As labor costs tend to account for the largest cost in healthcare, simply understanding the staff expense per provider is helpful in benchmarking across providers, practices and clinics. Staff expenses are more than just staff wages or salaries and include benefits and other staff expense perks. Establishing the right number of Staff FTE per provider FTE is critical to establishing a productive clinic and will be the largest driver for staff expense. Besides the number of staff per provider FTE, staff pay rate and staff benefits will drive the staff expense per provider FTE. (See Figure 22.4 on page 151.)

In many geographic areas, to get the best employees, pay, benefits, and perks must be set to attract strong front office and medical assistant staff. Keep in mind, organizations are not just competing against other healthcare organizations for resources, so the pay rates and benefits must be attractive enough.

What are the Work Relative Value Units (wRVUs) per Visit per Provider?

Each patient visit can carry different complexity and different amounts of workload. Work Relative Value Units (wRVUs) exist to categorize visits based on complexity and workload (see Figure 22.5 on page 152). In Fee for Service reimbursement, documented wRVUs for each visit drive reimbursement. One way to compare average workload, average complexity, and average reimbursement potential across providers, is by aggregating the average wRVU per visit by provider (see Figure 22.6 on page 153).

Labor Expenses per Provider FTE			
	Actual	**Budget**	**% Variance**
Staff Salaries & Wages	823,522	784,047	-5.0%
Employee Benefits	628,236	664,295	5.4%
Total Labor Expense	1,451,758	1,448,342	-0.2%
Provider FTE	8	8	0.0%
Staff FTE per Provider FTE	181,470	181,043	-0.2%

Figure 22.4   Shows the simple calculation for the staff expense per provider FTE based on the staff labor expenses (excludes provider pay). In this example, the clinic pays over $180,000 in labor expenses per each provider FTE it has on staff.

Keep in mind that wRVUs are driven by clinical documentation for charge purposes and documentation is sometimes completed in error or not completed adequately enough for this purpose. Knowingly documenting more than what was done for a visit is fraud because it increases the reimbursement per visit, though not all overdocumentation is a knowing misrepresentation, while under-documentation leads to less reimbursement.

What are the Days to Access Care?

The lead time from when an appointment is made until the appointment occurs is a retrospective key indicator for how long it takes patients to access care. The next or third next available appointment is the forward-looking method that also measures how long it takes patients to access care (see Figure 22.7 on page 154). Measuring and maintaining a simple running chart of both measures will help identify patient satisfaction and capacity issues for clinic leaders.

While day by day, these measures fluctuate, over an extended period of time, there will likely be a stable expected measure of access to care. If the stable expected time to access care is within the organization's standard of care, then great, but if not, then the organization should look for ways to improve. Once Patient Access measures begin to trend an increase in time, clinic leaders should assess problems with each provider's capacity and the overall total provider capacity, and scrutinize the underlying throughput

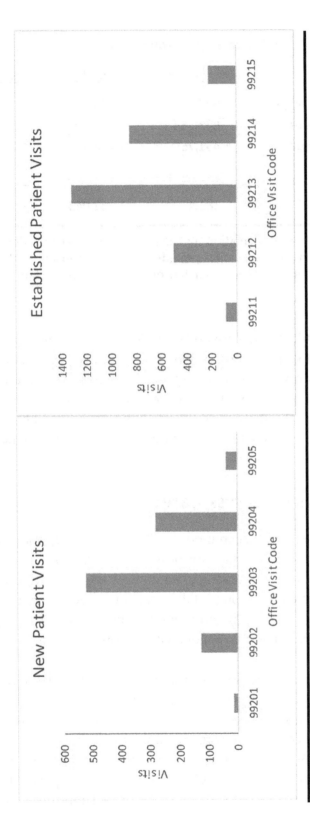

Figure 22.5 **The graphs are sample charts indicating what the office visit distribution may look like for a particular provider. Each office visit carries different relative value or weight, with 99201 and 99211 the lowest and 99205 and 99215 the highest.**

wRVU per Visit by Provider			
Provider	**Visits**	**Total wRVU**	**wRVU per Visit**
D. Jones, MD	4,532	4,897	1.1
J. Doe, MD	3,986	4,656	1.2
W. Smith, DO	5,163	4,811	0.9
A. Thomas, PA	5,432	5,321	1.0
L. King, CNP	4,100	4,200	1.0

Figure 22.6 The table shows the calculation for average wRVUs per visit for each provider. In this example, J. Doe has the highest wRVU per visit which tends to indicate that J. Doe receives more reimbursement on average per visit and each visit is slightly more complex. Of course, each payer plays a big role in actual reimbursement as does the degree to which a provider completes clinical documentation in generating wRVUs.

processes. In some situations, more efficiency in the processes leads to more patient throughput which subsequently drives down the time to access care, though at some point, provider capacity is the main barrier that must be addressed.

How Much Planned Provider Time is Lost or Unused?

Patients that are scheduled for appointments don't always show up and keep the scheduled appointment. When this happens, provider time is often lost to all patients unless the clinic double booked patients or a Same Day acute patient fills the available time. Patient "No Shows" or patients who do not keep appointments are important to track because these indicate lost provider capacity or a potential loss to provider capacity as well as system inefficiency. No shows are measured as a percentage of patients that schedule appointments but do not keep them and the higher the percentage, the worse the problem is for a clinic. If the number and percentage of No Shows is tracked, then clinic managers can estimate each provider's lost capacity and the potential number of lost visits can be derived (see Figure 22.8 on page 155).

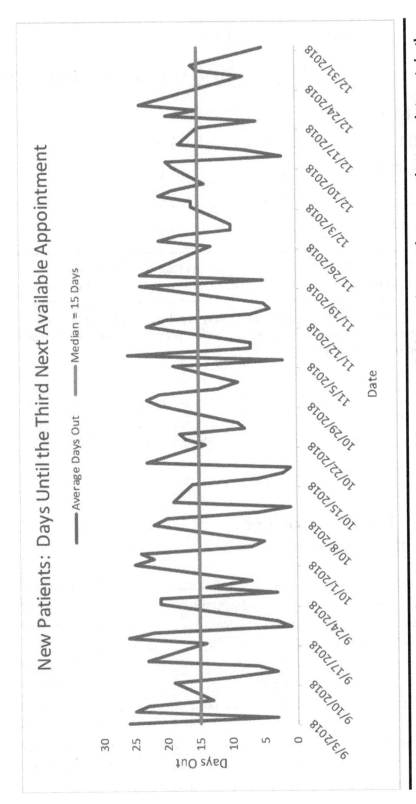

Figure 22.7 The run chart above shows the days until third next available appointment for new patient appointments in the last quarter of 2018. Each work day the days until the third next available appointment were captured and graphed. Overall the median time is 15 days, or new patients can expect to wait 15 days, though that varies day by day.

	No Shows
Scheduled Appointments	4,580
Completed Visits	3,664
No Shows	916
No Show Rate	20.0%
Lost Revenue $	87,020
	UnBooked
Available Hours to Schedule	1,560
Hours Booked for Patients	1,527
Unbooked Time	33
Unbooked Rate	2.1%
Missed Visits	99
Lost Revenue $	9,405

Figure 22.8   Shows the impacts of patient No Shows and unbooked available provider time. In the example above, a provider had 1,560 hours available to schedule patients in a year but only 1,527 of those hours were booked. In the 1,527 available hours booked, 4,580 appointments were scheduled but only 3,664 patients showed up. If nothing was done to counteract the lost capacity, then this provider lost a total of 338 patient care hours and 1,015 patient visits due to No Shows and unbooked time.

Provider schedules are frequently filled up and backlogged but sometimes provider schedules have openings. New providers or providers new to an area generally take time to build up a full schedule of patients, but established providers sometimes have gaps in their schedules too. A common occurrence is when patients cancel appointments within a week or two of the appointment and that time slot is at a less desirable time of the week, so the clinic scheduling staff do not fill the vacated appointment slot. Unbooked appointment slots are another measure that estimate each provider's lost capacity or potential loss. Unbooked slots are measured as a percentage of total schedule slots or unbooked time as a percentage of total available scheduled time.

How Long do Patients Wait?

Patients tend to not like waiting and the longer the wait the more frustrated patients become. The point at which wait is deemed excessive often varies by the type of patient, patient demographics, or patient experiences in other services in the local market. Wait time is generally measured as the amount of time a patient spends in the waiting room before rooming begins, though other considerations should be accounted for.

First, patients often wait in the exam room too. Once a patient is roomed and clinical support staff leave, there is routinely another round of wait that occurs before a provider first enters the exam room. Sometimes this wait is much longer than the wait occurring in the waiting room though it is not easily monitored or measured. This wait can often be more critical because patients are waiting in a more expensive exam room rather than a general waiting room and patients can often be forgotten when hidden in an exam room.

Second, in appointment driven clinics, true wait time is relative to how early patients arrive for the appointment compared to the appointment time. Some patients arrive early, some arrive on time, and some arrive late. If a clinic is running on time and patients show up on time or late, then wait time actually looks better, but if a clinic is running on time and patients arrive early, then wait time may seem excessive (see Figure 22.9 on page 157).

In appointment-based clinics, it is often helpful to clearly define what appointment time means to staff, providers and patients in order to improve the time patients show up. Appointment time is often not agreed upon within a clinic let alone having a universal definition across clinics. Appointment time tends to mean a) the time the patient should arrive at the clinic b) the time the patient will start the rooming process or c) the time the patient should expect the provider to walk in the exam room door for the first time. To improve processes related to scheduled appointment clinics, it is often preferable to have an "on time" measure instead of the wait time measure. An "on time" measure is simply the expected time a patient should arrive compared to actual time, or the expected time the patient should be in the exam room compared to actual time.

What are the Key Cycle Times of the Patient Flow Process?

While not necessarily the highest rating key measures, understanding the key cycle times of the patient care process is important for identifying delays, capacity constraints, benchmarking, and variation amongst

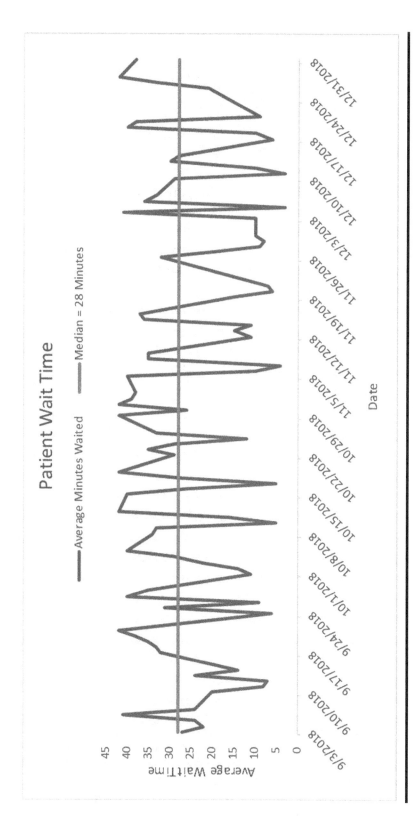

Figure 22.9 Is a run chart of patient wait time by date. Each day the average overall wait time is calculated and graphed on the run chart to see how normal the wait time appears because day by day it is normal to see some variation. In this case, the median patient wait time in the last quarter of 2018 is 28 minutes, so unless something changed, patients entering the clinic in 2019 can expect to wait 28 minutes, though day by day this will vary.

processes. Cycle time measures are useful in analyzing and redesigning patient flow processes.

First, learn how long it takes to check-in a patient once the patient is physically in the clinic. It is helpful to know how long the entire registration process takes if a patient completes much of the work remotely outside the clinic, but knowing the cycle time once the patient is in the clinic with clinic resources is more critical to patient flow design. Ideally check-in takes seconds or less than a few minutes.

Second, learn how long it takes to room the patient and complete diagnostics, discuss reason for visit, and update medication lists. This cycle time varies more than check-in but is often completed in under five to eight minutes. If staff complete more patient preparation tasks and complete more checks for the provider, or if a patient has more medications to reconcile than usual, this process will be longer.

Third, learn how long it takes for providers to see each patient and complete work for each patient during the clinic day. Provider cycle times vary by provider, reason for visit, and specialty. Another way to express this is by the inverse – the number of patients per hour a provider can see.

Fourth, learn how long discharge and check-out take. This cycle time should be relatively quick depending on how much appointment scheduling and education is provided to the patient. The longer this process takes, the more time resource is consumed in a busy exam room, a not so private check-out station, or at the busy check-in station.

	Accounting for Average Cycle Time			
		Hours	Visits	% of Available Capacity
1	Available Capacity	1,560	4,680	
2	Unbooked Capacity (-)	33	99	2.1%
3	Booked Capacity	1,527	4,581	97.9%
4	No Shows (-)	305	916	19.6%
5	Add Ons (+)	76	229	4.9%
6	Capacity Used	1,298	3,894	83.2%
7	Average Cycle Time	0.4		
8	Visits per Hour		2.5	

Figure 22.10 Breaks down a provider's overall average cycle time and accounts for unbooked time, no shows, and add on visits to impact the overall average cycle time. Even though an observation study indicates this provider sees patients for 20 minutes each, the real life adjustments show that the cycle time is 0.4 hours or roughly 24 minutes per patient. On average the provider sees 2.5 patients per hour.

CLOSING

Chapter 23

Conclusion and What's Next?

As simple as simple clinics sound, there are many nuances and variables to understand for each clinic and for clinics in general. There are countless differences between clinics to account for and underlying reasons for the differences to understand. There are seldom single right answers about the best thing to do or a single best way to do something in a clinic because the right answers depend on so many factors.

At the same time, there are some generalities that can be assessed in all clinics. There are core operating principles shared between all clinics and general processes all clinics follow. There are challenges all clinics face and opportunities all clinics can exploit.

The intent behind this book was not to be all things to all readers. The intent was for the materials in this book to provide a basic understanding to those new to clinic operations, a framework for management professionals to complete a basic assessment of any simple clinic, and a means to explain the fundamental challenges in clinics so that supporting professionals can learn to relate to them. At a minimum, I hope the book has provided some better questions to discuss with clinic staff, perhaps some useful example tables to better analyze clinic performance or to illustrate some findings, and maybe it has offered a refresher for those with extensive experience. This book is hopefully a good starting point for each reader to build from and seek more experiential learning.

The following appendix is a list of all the questions covered in this book. My recommendation is, the next time you have the chance to visit a clinic, see how many questions you can answer. If you have only 30 minutes in the clinic or if you have three days, see how much you can answer. Use the sample tables, graphs, and diagrams as examples to illustrate your understanding of the clinic. Compare what you find to outside research and what benchmarking organizations say is best practice. Compare what you find to other service experiences inside and outside healthcare. Once you have done this over and over again, the process will become second nature. Once experienced, each reader will be able to expand the knowledge base picked up along the way.

As for me, I plan to keep assessing, learning, updating this knowledge base, and using it in practical work. While work takes me into simple clinics frequently, I also find myself in more complex clinic systems, Emergency Departments, Surgical Departments, and other healthcare settings. Perhaps I will document what I have found in those as well.

Appendix A: Checklist of all Questions

SECTION II Overview on Clinics Including the People and Payers

Chapter 3 – General Questions to Help Understand a Clinic or Medical Practice

☐ Who are the Providers?
☐ Who are the Managers and Administrators?
☐ Who are the Clinical Staff?
☐ Who are the Support Staff?
☐ Who are the Patients?
☐ How is the Organization paid?
☐ What is the Payer Mix?

SECTION III Patient Throughput, Patient Flow, and Capacity

Chapter 4 – Questions to Understand How Patients Access Care or Patient Access

☐ What Type of Care do Patients Access?
☐ How do Patients Access Care?
☐ How Long do Patients Wait to Access Care?

Chapter 5 – Questions to Understand the Basics of the Clinic Capacity

- ☐ What Types of Point of Care Space Exist?
- ☐ How Many Point of Care Spaces Exist?
- ☐ What Hours of the Day and Days of the Week is the Clinic Open?
- ☐ How Many Providers are Working During which Hours and Days?
- ☐ How Many Providers are Working Compared to Space Available to Work?

Chapter 6 – Questions to Understand what Happens Before the Patient Visits

- ☐ How Much of the check-in, Registration, and Payment Processing can a Patient do Before Setting Foot in the Clinic?
- ☐ How Much Health Screening and Form Filling Out is Done in Advance?
- ☐ What Tasks do the Front Office do to Prepare for Each Patient that Visits?
- ☐ What Tasks do the Clinical Staff do to Prepare for Each Patient that Visits?
- ☐ What Tasks do Providers do to Prepare for Each Patient that Visits?

Chapter 7 – Questions to Understand Location of a Clinic and a Location Strategy for the Clinic

- ☐ Physically, Where is the Clinic Located?
- ☐ Physically, What Type of Space is it?
- ☐ How Accessible is the Clinic?
- ☐ What is the Market Competition Like in the Area?
- ☐ Is there a Location Strategy for the Clinic?

Chapter 8 – Questions to Understand how Patients Arrive and Register

☐ How do Patients Find Registration?
☐ Where and how do Patients Check-in?
☐ Is the Check-in Private?
☐ Does a Line Form and Where does it Form?
☐ Do Patients Check-out in the Same Spot?
☐ Do Patients Have to Fill out Paperwork?
☐ How Long does Check-in Take?
☐ How is the Waiting Room?

Chapter 9 – Questions to Understand how Patients get Roomed

☐ Are Patients Self-rooming?
☐ Who Escorts the Patient to a Patient Care Room?
☐ Where are Height, Weight, and Vitals Acquired?
☐ Who is Discussing a Patient's Reason for the Visit and Current medications?
☐ Are the Clinical Staff Working at the Top of Licensure?
☐ Are Patients Stopping for Collections First or at the End?
☐ How do the Clinical Staff Alert the Provider that the Patient is Ready?

Chapter 10 – Questions to Understand the Provider Exam and Provider Workflow

☐ How Much Time do Providers Spend in the Exam Room with Patients?

☐ How Much Documentation are Providers Completing in the exam Room with the Patient?

☐ How Much Time are Providers Spending in Motion between Exam Rooms?

☐ How Much Time are Providers Spending on Patient Care Tasks outside the Exam Room between Patients?

☐ Is the Exam Room Set up for Good Interaction between Patient and Caregiver?

☐ Do Providers Use Scribes, Dictation, or Voice Recognition?

☐ How does a Provider let Clinical Staff Know that they Need Something during an Exam?

☐ How does the Provider Give the Patient Closure?

Chapter 11 – Questions to Understand Patient Discharge and Patient Treatment

☐ Who Schedules Treatments, Follow-up Appointments, or Further Care for the Patient?

☐ Who Completes and Where are the After Visit Summary and Discharge Completed?

Chapter 12 – Questions to Understand Patient Care Happening Between Visits

☐ How are Refills Managed?

☐ Who Manages Email or Phone Traffic?

☐ How Much Outreach is Completed?

SECTION IV Key Concepts and Variables to Assess

Chapter 13 – Questions to Understand the Care Team

- ☐ Who is Part of the Care Team?
- ☐ How do the Providers Act as Part of the Larger Care Team?

Chapter 14 – Questions to Understand Patient Scheduling and Provider Schedules

- ☐ How Much Time do Providers Book for Each Visit or Allocate per Patient?
- ☐ How do Providers Schedule the Care Day?
- ☐ Is there a Difference between Time Scheduled or Allocated per Patient and What is Used?

Chapter 15 – Questions to Understand how the Provider is the Capacity Constraint

- ☐ What is the Typical Amount of Time a Provider Spends per Patient Visit?
- ☐ How Often do a Provider's Patients Visit?
- ☐ How Often or how many Hours a Year does a Provider See Patients?
- ☐ What is a Provider's Expected Capacity or Panel Size?
- ☐ What is a Provider's Actual Throughput and Panel Size?
- ☐ How many Hours do Providers Work Compared to What is Planned?

Chapter 16 – Questions to Understand the Total Provider Capacity

- ☐ Are "Extenders" Used?
- ☐ What is the Combined Panel Size for All Providers?

Chapter 17 – Questions to Understand how Physical Space is Used and Managed

☐ Who Preps Point of Care Space and Maintains the Rooms?
☐ How Flexible are Patient Care Rooms?
☐ How are Rooms Allocated to Providers?
☐ What is the Utilization of Patient Care Space?
☐ What is the Potential for any Underutilized Space?

Chapter 18 – Questions to Understand the Equipment and Technology Used

☐ What Electronic Registration Systems are Used?
☐ What Electronic Clinical Documentation Systems are Used?
☐ What System is Used for Scheduling?
☐ What Diagnostic and Clinic Equipment is Used?
☐ How is Technology Used?

SECTION V Key Infrastructure Concepts

Chapter 19 – Questions to Understand Leadership and Management Systems

☐ Who are the Formal Leaders in the Clinic or Practice?
☐ Who are the Informal Leaders in the Practice or Clinic?
☐ How is the Practice Managed?
☐ How Often are there All Staff Meetings and All Provider Meetings?
☐ How Often are there Team Huddles?
☐ How does the Practice Manager Engage with Support Teams?
☐ Are there Management Systems Like Lean in Place?

Chapter 20 – Questions to Understand the History of the Clinic

☐ Was the Practice Acquired by a Larger Health System?
☐ Was the Practice Formed from Disparate Provider Practices?
☐ How Many and Which Providers have been in Private Practice?

Chapter 21 – Questions to Understand the Strategy and Overall Challenges to Consider

☐ What is the Role of the Clinic?
☐ What Strategies does the Clinic Deploy and are they Aligned with the Purpose?

Chapter 22 – Questions to Understand the Key Measurements

☐ What is the P&L?
☐ What is the Bottom Line per Provider per Year?
☐ How Many Staff FTEs are there per Provider?
☐ What is the Staff Expense per Provider FTE?
☐ What are the Work Relative Value Units (wRVUs) per Visit per Provider?
☐ What are the Days to Access Care?
☐ How Much Planned Provider Time is Lost or Unused?
☐ How Long do Patients Wait?
☐ What are the Key Cycle Times of the Patient Flow Process?

Index

Page numbers in *italics* denote figures.